InLace™ Techniques
Resin Inlay for Gourd and Wood Crafts

Betsey Sloan

Photography by Jennifer Van Allen

Schiffer Publishing Ltd®

4880 Lower Valley Road, Atglen, Pennsylvania 19310

Dedication

This book is dedicated to Judy Briscoe,
of Englewood, Florida.
Judy was there when I opened my first gourd and
drilled my first antler. Her ongoing encouragement of
my work and teaching will always be appreciated.

Copyright © 2009 by Betsey Sloan
All photos copyright © by Jennifer Van Allen unless otherwise
noted. Cover: Large gourd done by Gloria Cranes.
Library of Congress Control Number: 2009925835

Designed by "Sue"
Type set in NewBskvll BT

ISBN: 978-0-7643-3330-9
Printed in China

Published by Schiffer Publishing, Ltd.
4880 Lower Valley Road
Atglen, PA 19310
Phone: (610) 593-1777; Fax: (610) 593-2002
E-mail: Info@schifferbooks.com

For our complete selection of fine books on this and related subjects, please visit our website at www.schifferbooks.
com. You may also write for a free catalog.

This book may be purchased from the publisher. Please
try your bookstore first.

We are always looking for people to write books on new
and related subjects. If you have an idea for a book, please
contact us at proposals@schifferbooks.com.

Schiffer Publishing's titles are available at special dis-
counts for bulk purchases for sales promotions or premiums.
Special editions, including personalized covers, corporate
imprints, and excerpts can be created in large quantities for
special needs. For more information, contact the publisher.

CONTENTS

My first can of InLace®, purchased in 2004, sat unopened in my studio for several years, well past the suggested shelf life. What kept me from opening and using that can was plain old fear. While I understood the basic concepts of using the resin, lingering questions plagued me. How deep is the carving in the gourd supposed to be? Should I have bought more colors or additives? What is the mixture supposed to look like? How do I transfer a liquid mixture and keep it in a carving on a curved surface? What do I use to grind the inlay down and what compounds work to polish it?

In 2007, I was fortunate to obtain a job with Turtle Feathers, an art supply company that carries the entire InLace product line. My first project, to be used as a marketing tool, was to create fifteen samples of each color mix and the clear formula, with all the dyes. One of those samples could have an additional element, such as metallic dust or stone flakes. Talk about a fast learning curve. And I will admit that not everything went as planned during that initial project. The second batch never set. I forgot to add the hardener!

I began teaching InLace classes around the country as I traveled with Turtle Feathers to various gourd events. What I discovered was that a lot of gourd artisans had the very same concerns about InLace that I initially had. How great it was to see the relief on their faces as they found out how easy it was to use the resin. These two things, combined, led me to writing a book about using InLace.

There is one key ingredient to working with In-Lace—and that is patience. The process, from carving the gourd through the final polish of the inlay, cannot be rushed.

However, even as an instructor of InLace, the product can create challenges. Read on.

A Design with a Life of its Own

This image, "Dancing in the Gourd Patch," is an example of having multiple carvings in a design and using InLace all around the gourd, but it also shows the problems encountered when the "design" element takes on a life of it's own.

I bought this gourd in Ohio while attending the gourd gathering. Things were slow at the vending booth due to classes, so I began sketching a few chunky ladies surrounding the gourd. Soon I was drawing a "road" for them to dance on and created a top line so they all were the same height. Then I spaced them out, all with their hands touching, left and right.

I knew I wanted to use InLace on each of the figures, so over the course of the next few months, whenever I had the time, I would carve out a design in the dresses. Soon, they were ready to have the inlays.

Even though I had access to a lot of InLace dusts, flakes, and dyes, somehow my color choices always reverted to my safety zone…blue, green, and purple. As you can see in the photo, I didn't deviate much.

With a design like this — going all the way around the gourd — I had to inlay each lady separately.

When this was all done, over the course of another few months, it was time to woodburn the figures and then start the grinding/sanding process.

When I was sanding, I was so eager to get it done, that I took off too much gourd skin from around several of the figures. Sometimes this can be fixed, but not this time. I hadn't noticed when I bought the gourd (I just loved the shape!) that the skin was very dry and had a lot of mottled areas. As I started to add the base stain to the gourd (I use Tria alcohol inks), the dryness, mottled areas, and my skinned spots just didn't look right.

Out came the carver and my favorite ball bit. I decided to carve around all the figures so that they were dancing around the gourd within this carved area. Take a look at the photo—it was very hard carving around the skinny arms and hands, but finally, I got all the figures carved out and all the gourd skin around and between them removed.

The author's "Dancing Ladies" went through many changes before finally locating themselves in the gourd patch.

Hummmmm. I didn't like the spaces between the ladies and the bareness of the carving under and over them, so I started a filigree design. Nope, too fussy with so much area. So I put a textured carbide drill bit on my Optima and started to shape gourds and gourd leaves behind the ladies. Thus the name, "Dancing in the Gourd Patch."

But wait, I'm not done. I initially had painted the "gourd patch" a greenish color with some green Interference paint as highlights. While in that format, it won a blue ribbon at the local fair—yet I still wasn't comfortable with it. Out came a shade of blue acrylic paint. Ugh. Too light and that particular brand of paint didn't want to go over the spar varnish that I had used as a final coat. So I bought some navy acrylic paint and that covered ALL the colors eventually. If you've ever painted a filigree design, you know how hard it is to get a brush in that little hole in order to paint the edges of the carving!

While trying to cover the green with blue, I noted that some of the InLace inlays had scratches in them where I had rushed the hand-sanding. So I tried to hand-sand the inlays and while doing that, I found I didn't like the way I had woodburned around the inlay and parts of the design. Out came the rotary sander and the entire design was reduced, removing all the

woodburning lines and smoothing out the InLace. Of course, this also reduced the rise of the carved figures, so I had to re-carve them all over again.

In order to blend all those existing colors in the background, I still used some Interference green as highlights on the rounded gourds and a deeper green on the leaves. When done, the gourd looked like it was meant to have all those shades in it.

If there is a moral here, it's to take time up-front. InLace, carving, and even coloring gourds can't be rushed. Now "Dancing" is one of my favorite pieces, and I have to laugh every time I look at the chunky ladies in their gourd patch.

As a gourd artisan and instructor, I have always shared tips, techniques, and sources. I hope that after reading this book you can approach InLace with new insight, confidence, and understanding about the endless possibilities that can be created with this decorative material.

I thank the artisans who supported this book with articles and photographs, and for being so willing to share their knowledge. A special thanks to the folks at Schiffer Publishing for helping me "build" the book, and to Jackie Jurecek for her endless support and assistance.

Enjoy.

Chapter One

WHAT IS INLACE?

InLace is a line of acetone-based resin, or plastic, products designed to work together to produce decorative inlays. First used as a substance to make eyeglass frames, the products soon came to the attention of woodcrafters and wood turners. These artisans were among the first to apply the resins in carved or recessed areas in bowls, goblets, guitars, pipes, cabinetry, tabletops, and other furniture. Eventually gourd artists discovered the product and today, many use the inlay material in any number of exciting ways. Even though some of the products in the InLace family use words like metallic or stone, the products are not metal or stone, but plastic, specifically designed to work together.

Because it is acetone based, InLace should always be mixed in paper or glass containers; one-ounce paper cups is the preferred choice for ease in measuring and simple clean up. Wooden mixing sticks, available at stores that carry craft products, are the preferred mixing tool.

InLace requires an activator, or hardener, to harden the mix. The time to fully harden an inlay can vary depending on temperature, humidity, and the amount of activator used.

There are hundreds of color and texture combinations available with InLace that add excitement to carved designs. A design might be as simple as a band around the top of a gourd, or a cabochon as part of an overall design. Or the design may be as complicated as having the entire carving inset with the resin. Taken one step further, the inlay itself can be carved. In the Gallery section there are many photos illustrating how InLace is used in gourd art and woodturning.

InLace does not absorb moisture and does not shrink or expand, with the exception of the clear formula, which may shrink slightly if no additives are used. InLace does settle into a carving so it is necessary to work with the mixture for a few minutes to ensure that a correct level is achieved, slightly higher than the surrounding gourd skin.

Shelf life is approximately one-year in a controlled environment. Avoid sunlight, heat, sparks, and flames. Be sure to read the section on Warnings and Precautions before working with InLace. Once opened, can rims should be kept clean and lids securely replaced. If crystals form at the rim and in the can, the mixture is no longer viable. If the mixture becomes slightly thick in the can, a little acetone may be used. If it has thickened to a point where it can't be stirred, then it's no longer usable.

InLace Products is the manufacturer and worldwide distributor of the InLace product line. Be sure to read the Resource section in the back of this book to help you locate suppliers of the products as well as sources for tools and equipment that will prove helpful in working with InLace.

The InLace product line is extensive and includes additives to enhance color, tone, and texture.

The products that make up the InLace family are extensive and you can get as elaborate or as simple as your budget allows. The heart of the line consists of 10 basic color mixtures and a clear formula. Seven of the color mixtures have tiny color chips in them that create tone and texture. The remaining three mixtures are solid, or opaque.

When I started teaching InLace classes, I searched for a word that would help me identify those first seven mixtures as a group, rather than using all seven names assigned to them. I settled on the word "premixed." This word won't be found on any packaging for InLace or on any promotional material or on web sites. I do use the term in this book because it assists me in explaining why texture and consistency are important, and which color mixtures are better than others for beginners to use. The word will just be our little secret.

Additives in the product line include InLace dyes in metallic, solid/opaque, and pearlescent; metallic dusts; stone flakes; nuggets; and granules.

The final four products in the line are the InLace hardener, or activator; Thicken-it, used to do just that, thicken a mixture; and two InLace compounds, one for buffing and one for polishing the inlay.

InLace is available in boxed kits that contain four-ounce or eight-ounce cans of the ten colors, or eight-ounces and sixteen-ounces of clear. Each kit contains a can of InLace, paper cups, mixing sticks, the correct amount of hardener for the size kit, and directions. Be sure to read the directions for precautions, warnings, and safe handling of InLace.

Basic Mixtures

Premixed InLace Colors

Beek

Lindsey

Becca

Scott

Lacey

Terra

The seven color mixtures that comprise the premixed InLace line are Becca, Beek, Lacey, Lindsey, Scott, Terra, and Turquoise. The tiny color chips that create these mixtures range from black, orange, and blue to red, green, and white, depending on the desired tone. The following chart shows premixed InLace colors in the can. The color chips on the can lid show the mixture hardened, but not sanded or polished.

Turquoise

Solid/Opaque InLace Colors

Solid/opaque InLace resins come in black, red, and white. These colors are thinner in texture than the premixed because they contain no additional color chips—just a dye to give them their opaque appearance. Solid/opaque colors can be used as they come from the can, or with color and texture additives. For use in gourd carvings, the solid/opaque InLace mixes always need a special InLace thickener.

Black

White

Red

Clear InLace

The final basic resin in the InLace family is clear. This mixture has no colors or other additives. Clear InLace has a blue tint, but it hardens clear. And because it has no texture, to use with gourd carvings, color and texture need to be added by using any of the other InLace additives. Clear is practically impossible to keep in a carving because of its liquidness, so Thicken-it should always be added to Clear InLace.

Clear

InLace Dyes

Dyes in the InLace family are very intense, saturated colors that are used to create a color in clear or white InLace, or to shift or tone an existing color mixture. Before using, InLace dye needs to be well mixed. InLace dyes, in one-ounce jars, come in three categories: metallic, pearlescent, and solid/opaque. The bottles pictured below show the intensity of the color, and the small round disc shows that color added to and hardened in Clear InLace.

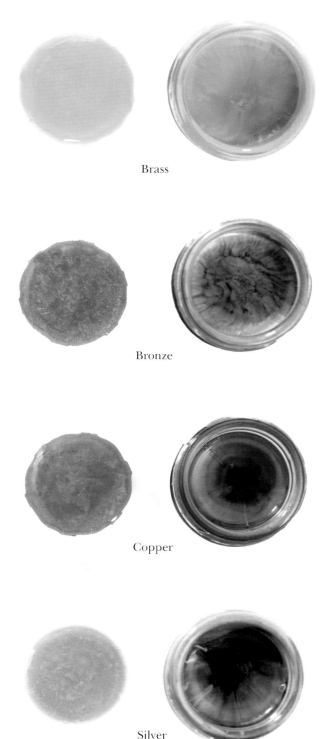

Brass

Bronze

Copper

Silver

Blue Pearl

Gold Pearl

Green Pearl

Red Pearl

White Pearl

Metallic InLace Dyes

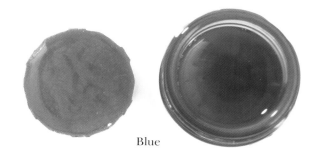

Blue

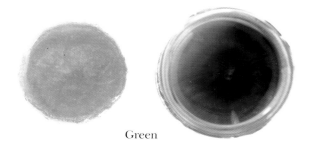

Green

Red Russet

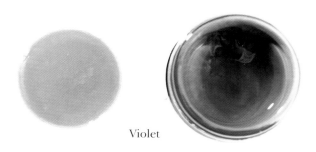

Violet

Solid/Opaque InLace Dyes

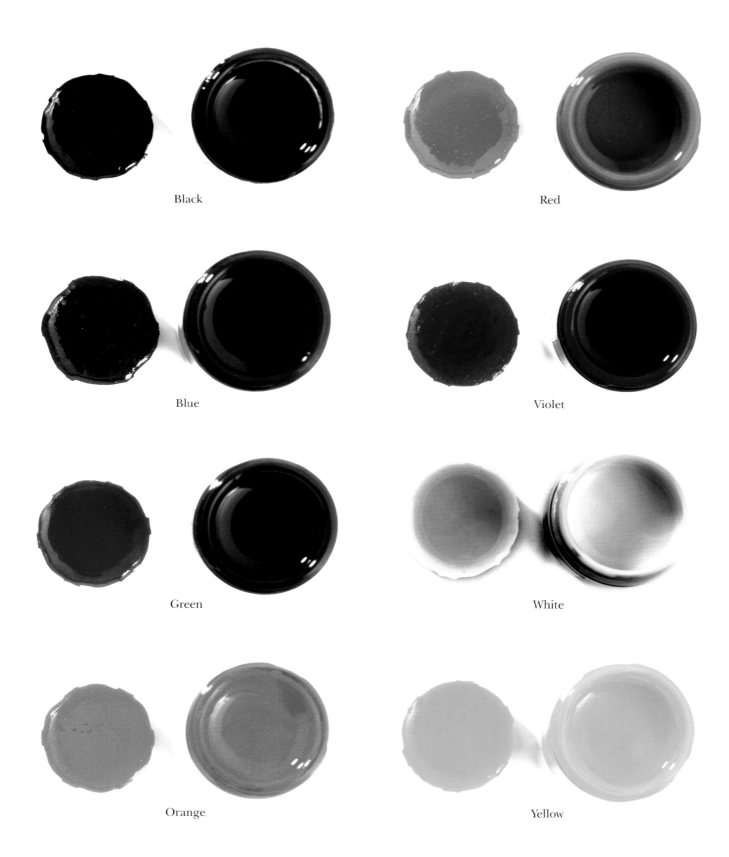

Black

Red

Blue

Violet

Green

White

Orange

Yellow

Decorative Materials

Metallic InLace Dust

Metallic dusts can add glitter to any inlay and are available in 15-dram vials.

Metallic InLace Dust adds a sparkle to any InLace resin. Small amounts at a time are added and then well mixed. The ratio of initial resin mixture to additives is 50/50. Adding too much can make the resin too thick to flow properly—AND WILL INHIBIT PROPER HARDENING. Metallic dusts are available in 15-dram vials.

Green

Maroon

Orange

Penny Copper

Purple

Red

Silver

Violet

Aqua

Black

Blue

Gold

InLace Stone Flakes

Stone Flakes add depth and texture. Twenty-four colors are available in 15-dram vials.

The line of stone flakes (remember, these are resin products, not real stone) in the InLace family is very colorful. Flakes can add depth and tone to a mixture and also help to slightly thicken the resin, but use the stone flakes sparingly because too much can make the mixture too thick and it won't flow into the corners of a design or into small areas. Stone flakes are available in 15-dram vials.

Butterscotch

Dark Chocolate

Cantaloupe

Deep Forrest Green

Aqua Pools

Caution Orange

Electro Blue

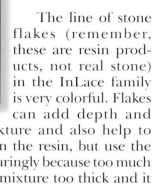

Baby Blue

Brick House

Coco

Gray Fox

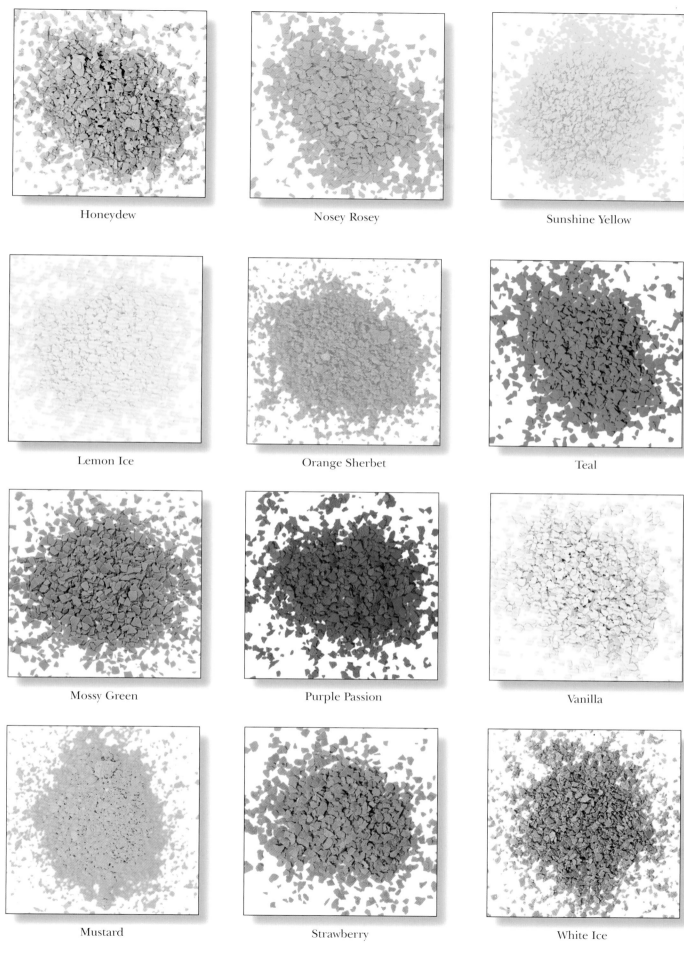

Honeydew

Nosey Rosey

Sunshine Yellow

Lemon Ice

Orange Sherbet

Teal

Mossy Green

Purple Passion

Vanilla

Mustard

Strawberry

White Ice

InLace Nuggets

Adding nuggets to an InLace mixture can provide texture, tone, and color. However, add too many nuggets and the mix may be too thick to flow properly. Some gourd artists hand-place the larger nuggets directly into the inlay once the mixture has been placed into the carving, but before it starts to harden. This can be tricky especially if the inlay area is on a gourd curve as opposed to a flatter section. It takes good timing and control. No matter how they are added, the chunks of nugget, once polished, add a pleasing element to any design. Nuggets are available in two sizes, a four-ounce (by weight) jar and a ¾ ounce trial size.

CAUTIONARY NOTE: It is very important to keep in mind the 50/50 ratio when using InLace products. The base product (Clear, Lacey, Black, Turquoise, etc.) needs to comprise 50 percent or more of the final mixture once additives (flakes, dye, nuggets, etc.) are added. Going over the ratio of additives to mixture will inhibit the flow of the material and may cause the entire mix to remain sticky and not harden sufficiently to grind and polish.

Black

Blue

Bright Red

Brown

Gold

InLace Nuggets, in 16 colors, are available in four-ounce jars and ¾-ounce trial packets.

Gray

Sandalwood

Honeydew

Teal

Red Brown

Turquoise

Rose

White

Red Rust

InLace Granules

The InLace Granule product line contains the same colors and sizes as nuggets, so there is no need to repeat the color blocks. However, you will notice in the photo that the texture of the granules is much finer than that of nuggets. The same theory applies; add sparingly to allow the mixture to flow into the carving areas. Take care with handling InLace granules. They are fine plastic particles and should not be inhaled. Wearing a protective mask is always a good idea.

♥♥♥♥♥♥♥

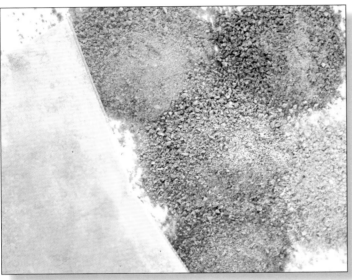

Granules are finer in texture than the InLace Nuggets, but the color pallet is the same.

Other Products

Thicken-it

This product provides substance, or thickness, to thin InLace mixtures. It should always be used with Clear InLace, as well as the solid/opaque formulas. I typically add a small amount of Thicken-it to all the premixed colors, too. Understanding the correct consistency/thickness of InLace is discussed in more detail in the Mixing chapter.

Take care when removing the lid from the Thicken-it jar, and when adding it to InLace resins. Thicken-it is very light and fluffy so avoid inhaling the small, white flakes. Again, a protective mask should always be used.

Thicken-it is a necessary addition to Clear InLace and most of the color mixtures.

Hardener

InLace Hardener is an activator that, once added, will begin the hardening process. Refer to the chart called Ratio of Hardener to InLace Mix located in the Mixing InLace section of this book for guidance. There are safety precautions, also, in using the activator. Be sure to read the warnings and precautions that come with each kit of InLace. The hardener is the last product to be added to the resin mix—just before inseting into a carving.

The activator that hardens the inlay mixtures is called InLace Hardener. Containers and special caps come with every kit of InLace and may also be purchased separately.

Compounds

There are two specific InLace compounds designed to work on the inlay once it has been ground and sanded to the appropriate level. The first is a brown-colored buffing compound, used to reduce scratches made in the sanding process. The second is a white polishing compound that highlights any remaining scratches, indents, or hills that might have been barely visible and, finally, shines the inlay. Both compounds are available in four-ounce sizes and are often offered at a discount if purchased with Thicken-it.

♥♥♥♥♥♥♥

Two compounds are available to buff and polish InLace. They are specifically designed to work with the resin inlays.

Warnings and Precautions

Be sure to read the directions and safety precautions included in every InLace kit. And refresh the memory by reading them each time InLace is used. Here are the most important things to remember.

1. Avoid eye contact, wear protective glasses, especially when grinding and polishing. In the event of eye contact, flush with plenty of water immediately and call a doctor.
2. Contact with skin should be avoided.
3. Keep InLace materials out of the sun and in an environment less than 72 degrees. Keep away from sparks and open flames.
4. Mix in glass or paper containers—never plastic or foam.
5. Keep the lid of the resin cans clean and close containers securely to prolong shelf life.
6. Use acetone to clean can rims and for general cleaning up.
7. Work in a well-ventilated area.
8. Wear a dust mask or a preferred small particle respirator when grinding and polishing.
9. Be careful when counting out drops of hardener. Never allow the entire bottle to be dumped into a mix. Excessive amounts of hardener-to-mix ratio, for instance 60 drops instead of six, can result in heat and possible injury or fire.

Chapter Three:

TOOLS AND EQUIPMENT

Basic Supplies

Here is a list of the basic items you should have on hand in order to easily work with InLace. Some items may already be around the house and in your studio; others may need to be purchased.

- acetone
- wooden mixing sticks*
- rags
- screwdriver and hammer
- safety glasses
- rotary carving tool
- assorted drill bits, felt or muslin wheels
with mandrel
- assorted sanding drums with mandrel
- paper plates
- one-ounce paper cups*
- dust mask or respirator
- sanding sponges or sandpaper
- toothpicks
- Q-tips with one end cut at an angle

*These two items come with InLace kits, but always have more available.

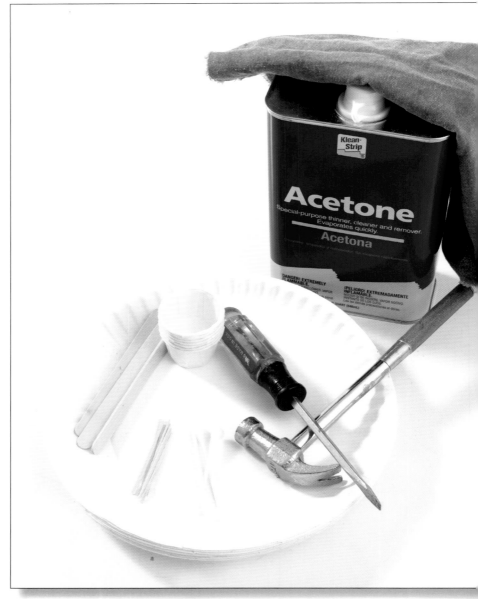

Having the right working materials is necessary for any project. Shown here are some of the suggested supplies needed to work with InLace.

Rotary Tools

While some gourd artists prefer to use hand-held gouges to carve gourds, most prefer using rotary tools. There are many types of rotary tools available to the gourd artist. The type used will depend on several things. First is the budget and second, how much carving is going to be accomplished over time. If carving gourds is going to be a once-in-a-while thing, then a cordless or less expensive electric tool is fine. If carving is going to be an important part of your gourd art, investing in a high quality tool is essential. Electric style rotary tools, like Dremel®, Foredom®, and Optima®, reduce hand and wrist fatigue because they operate at a higher rotation per minute and have less vibration than a cordless. At the high end of the carving spectrum is the air turbine for ultimate detail and control.

Try to "test drive" the different rotary tools before buying. Perhaps a friend has a rotary tool in their studio. Ask to use it for a few minutes and evaluate how the handpiece feels in your hand. Visit a gourd gathering where vendors will be happy to demonstrate their tools. Do some research and find the best fit for your budget.

I use an Optima 2, priced at about $320, for most of my intricate carving. It has no vibration and I can carve for hours. I also have a Dremel with a flexi-shaft to use when I want to remove large areas of the gourd surface. Dremels can run anywhere from $25 to $95 depending on the accessories. Don't be misled by the offer of a lot of accessories with some of the rotary kits. Most bits that come with a typical rotary tool kit are intended for general household use and are unsuitable for gourd carving.

Any of the flexi-shaft rotary tools are beneficial, but be sure to purchase a hanging stand for the body of the tool, or make something so the body hangs above you and the shaft is allowed to run without bending. If the shaft continually binds, it's easy to burn out the motor.

Foredom rotary tools, complete with flexi-shafts and hand pieces, are priced between $285 and $375. Air turbines run between $275 and $570. A list of suppliers for all these rotary tools can be found in the Resource section located in the final pages of this book.

Pictured with the Dremel and my Optima is a small rotary tool I picked up at the Florida Gourd Show many years ago. It is just a wonderful back-up tool and cost $29. I wouldn't carve an entire gourd with it, but for touch up and small jobs it works fine.

A rotary tool is the most common way to prepare a gourd to accept an inlay. Several types are available, as shown here.

Regardless of what type of rotary tool is purchased, with the exception of rotary tools like the Optima 2 that has an open/close system for bits, one additional purchase is a small item called a Universal Chuck®. This $10 item is worth its weight in gold when it comes to changing bits. The Universal is placed on the end of a rotary tool and is simply opened and closed to accommodate a variety of bit sizes. There is no longer any need for digging through that toolbox to find the right sized collets that matches the next bit to be use

An extremely handy item to use with a rotary tool is the Universal Chuck. It replaces the need for various sizes of collets and makes bit changing much easier.

Masks, Respirators, and Safety Glasses

It is essential that a mask or respirator be worn when grinding and polishing InLace and when using Thicken-it. The plastic particles removed by the sanding drums and other grinding tools should not be inhaled or allowed to drift into the eyes. Paper masks that have a metal strip that is shaped over the nose are not recommended. Paper masks that have a small filter device in the center are better, but not for long-term carving. Best are small-particle respirators. I refer to them as "Star Wars" masks. They take a little getting used to, but before long, the clean air that comes through the mask is much appreciated. Likewise, eye protection is mandatory, especially the type that fits over the entire eye.

Protection from gourd or wood dust, especially while carving, is essential. A high quality face mask can guard against inhaling the by-products.

Optional Equipment

If you're going to be doing a lot of carving, a dust collector is a great investment. I was shocked to see the amount of dust that was drawn into the collector the first time I used it. Check various models to see how quietly they run, whether or not they have handy outlets on the side, and if they have adjustable side and top pieces that can be used to "build" a frame around the gourd while carving. A homemade dust collector can also be created by using a small shop vacuum and a cardboard box.

The final tool for consideration is a rotary sander. There are many models available like Microlux® and Craftsmen®. While these sanders make short work in reducing the initial inlay, it's very easy to over-sand and wipe out the gourd skin as well, leaving a demarcation line around the inlay. In some cases, this is not a problem and may even be desired as part of the design element. The trick is to keep the sander level with the surface of the gourd as it reduces the bulk of the inlay—and to stop grinding before the sanding discs reach the gourd skin.

There are several optional tools that make the carving process easier and safer. Shown here are a dust collector and several styles of rotary sanders.

Drill Bits

There are numerous bits that can be used with gourd carving, from dental to engraving, from textured carbide to high-speed steel. Diamond bits are not recommended except for smoothing down carvings once the skin is removed. High-speed steel bits are inexpensive and come in a wide variety of shapes and sizes. There are three basic shapes recommended for beginning carvers: the wheel, a ball, and either a cylinder or inverted cone. What is purchased will depend on the type of carving to be accomplished: either very fine detail or large inlay areas. Shank diameter of the bits will depend on the type of rotary tool being used. Check the instructions that come with the rotary tool for recommendations.

Carbide bits are more expensive than steel bits, but will stay sharper longer. When budget is a consideration, stick with high-speed steel. The exception is the purchase of at least one structured tooth carbide bit. These bits are invaluable in removing large quantities of gourd material quickly and for shaping and rounding design areas. They have sharp hair-like projections protruding from all sides rather than the cutting flutes found in the steel bits. Structured tooth carbide bits are available in ball, cone, flame, and cylinder.

Since I'm basically self-taught, I started with only three different sizes of steel ball bits. But now my collection is more diverse. While there are many types of drill bits available, the following is what I consider the basic set.

A basic bit set may include those shown here, bottom, left to right: textured carbide ball, two sizes of inverted cones and three sizes of ball bits. Back row: pointed bit and two sizes of wheel bits.

1. Inverted Cones are used to remove a lot of gourd pulp quickly, usually from larger areas to be carved. When held on end, they will provide a slightly angled, concave edge to a carving.

2. Ball bits range from the small engraving ball to larger sizes and are useful in shaping and removing pulp from under the gourd skin when creating an undercut. I also use a small engraving bit to clean up the edges of a carved design as a final step **before** insetting the inlay material.

3. Wheel bits take a little getting used to. They can have a mind of their own, so control of the hand piece is essential. The wheel is used to outline the areas to be carved. It creates a crisp, deep line around the design, making it easier to remove the gourd material. With care, the wheel can also be used to square corners.

4. Textured carbide bits can make quick work in removing large areas from a design. They are also useful for shaping and rounding.

5. A straight tipped bit, either steel or engraving, is very useful to square corners. I like to have at least one available when carving.

As with all new tools, practice makes perfect. Test any newly purchased bit on a thick gourd scrap rather than a real design. Get the feel for how the bit grabs the gourd skin and underneath pulp and determine the best use for the bit: smoothing, removing, or shaping. There is more information on techniques for using bits in the Carving section.

Grinding, Sanding, and Polishing Tools

There are many helpful hints on the entire process of grinding, sanding, and polishing in that chapter, including suggested grits. The first task is to reduce the inlay by sanding the hardened mixture down to just above the gourd skin level and without nicking the skin. Most gourd artists accomplish this with sanding drums. The drums slip onto a mandrel and are then inserted into any type of rotary tool and used on low speed.

Next, it's time to switch to hand-sanding—sanding the inlay by hand reduces the inlay to gourd skin level, removing any hills and remaining rough spots or gouges made by the sanding drums. While I prefer the sponge sandpaper because it can be wound around a finger in order to control pressure and direction, others may prefer a sanding block, regular sandpaper, or even stone bits. Also useful are sanding sticks for reaching tight spaces.

Sanding sponges, blocks, and sandpapers in grits ranging from medium coarse to micro fine are used to hand-sand inlays following the initial reduction.

Felt or muslin wheels, mounted on a mandrel and inserted into a rotary tool, are used to buff and polish the inlay. Always on low speed, the felt/muslin wheels push the compounds into the inlay, removing slight scratches and then raising a shine.

Sanding tools include mandrels with various sizes and grits of sanding drums, initially used to reduce the hardened inlay.

To buff and polish inlays, either felt or muslin wheels mounted on a mandrel and used with a rotary tool, are suggested.

It's important to understand that the following chapters are written from my perspective and based on experience as well as talking with other gourd artisans. Gourd instructors develop their own style of explaining things and can even differ in techniques and what equipment to use. This is not a bad thing. It just means that we have all reached the same conclusion from different paths. As long as the basic safety precautions are met and the general guidelines in the following sections are used, the end result will be a wonderful, colorful, well-produced inlay.

The Process

So, the reading has been done on all the InLace family of products, the first kit of InLace purchased, and the tools and equipment gathered. Now what? Basically, here is the process that is explained in depth in the following sections and chapters:

1. Select a good, thick gourd with an outer skin that will enhance the design.

2. Select and transfer a design, having a clear understanding of which areas are to be inlaid. Do not paint/stain any of the gourd at this stage.

3. Carve the inlay areas.

4. Select InLace products, mix in a paper cup, add hardener, and insert into the carving.

5. Let the mixture harden, between 12 and 24-hours.

6. Reduce the inlay with a rotary tool and sanding drums to just above gourd skin level.

7. Hand-sand with sanding sponges/sandpaper to gourd skin level.

8. Buff to remove scratches.

9. Polish to shine.

10. Submit the inlay to the sunlight test.

11. Repeat from number seven. What? Yes, repeat the hand-sanding through polishing. This is typical. I often go back to the hand sanding process three or four times before I'm satisfied.

12. Add a coat of any varnish or acrylic finish to the inlay area as protection.

13. Finish the design if required. Add woodburning, any colorants, etc. to the gourd.

14. Apply a final finish and add rim embellishments if desired.

♥♥♥♥♥♥♥

Carving the Gourd

Selecting the Perfect Gourd

To accept and hold the InLace mixture securely, the depth of the carved area in a gourd needs to be at least 1/8th of an inch deep. Selecting a thick gourd is essential. Some gourd vendors can provide thick gourds if that is specified, but the best way to get them is to select them personally. Use your knuckles to knock on the gourd. Thick gourds make a lower resonating sound when knocked; thinner gourds have a higher tone. Most gourd artists develop "educated knuckles" over time. And a thick gourd just plain feels heavier than a thinner one.

Selecting a thick gourd makes carving inlays much easier. Here are two examples of gourds with sufficient thickness.

Carving the Design

First, remove all jewelry from hands and wrists, and don't wear a shirt that is very loose as it can get caught in the rotary tool handpiece (been there, done that). Now, you need to transfer a design onto the gourd surface, either free-hand or traced, using graphite or carbon paper. Also used to transfer designs are pyrography paper and household stretch and seal plastic products. Read further before woodburning the design in advance of carving. If my design consists entirely of InLace, then I woodburn in order to have a line to follow while carving out the inlay area. But, if the inlay is to be **part** of an overall wood-burned design, then I typically do not burn at this time. The reason for delaying the burn is if the drill bit gets a little frisky and goes outside the designated carved area, I can always adjust the pencil line. By woodburning first, if the carving goes outside what has been designated, I need to get really creative in changing the burned lines.

Overhand and Pencil Grips

There are two basic ways to hold a handpiece; the overhand grip and the pencil grip. The overhand grip uses the thumb as the resting point on the gourd while the fingers wrap around the handpiece and provide control of the bit. It takes a little practice to feel comfortable with this grip. The overhand grip is particularly useful when making long, sweeping cuts.

The pencil grip is just that — holding the handpiece in the same way a pencil is held. The pencil grip allows for more control when carving small areas, corners, making undercuts, and cleaning up the carving edges. Some rotary tools, like pistol shaped cordless ones, can only be held one way, the pencil grip. Likewise, older Dremel bodies are so bulky that they need the overhand grip in order to balance them in the hand. Newer model rotary tools, with smaller handpieces, allow for either grip.

Techniques for Carving

How large or small the carved design is to be will determine how many of the following steps are done. If the carved area is very small and intricate, there may be no need, or room, for the inverted cone or the larger ball bit as suggested in the following text. Common sense will dictate the steps required for each design. Assume we are doing a medium-sized dragonfly design in the following directions.

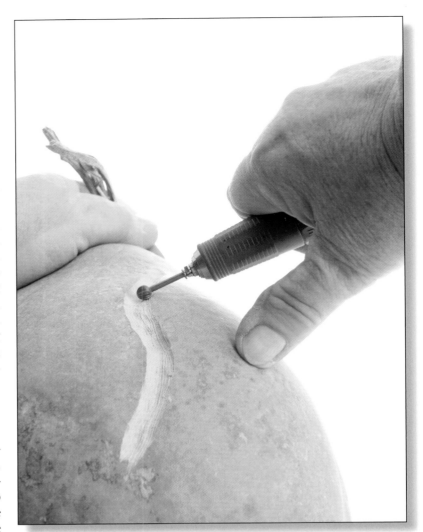

The overhand grip on a rotary tool or handpiece balances the hand on the thumb. The remainder of the hand controls direction and pressure of the bit as it carves.

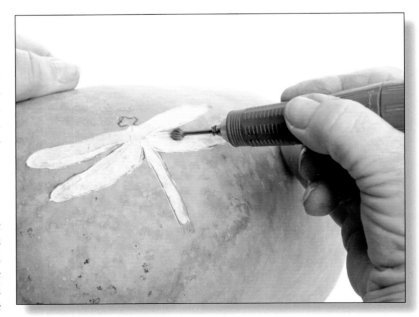

The pencil grip is used for most intricate carving when control of the bit is essential. The balance of the hand is created by the little finger and side of the hand.

1. The first step in carving a gourd is to outline the area to be carved with a wheel bit. Use the overhand grip and allow the wheel to mark the major lines of the design. Don't worry about tight corners or very curvy lines right now. If you're not comfortable with the wheel bit and need more practice, simply start with the second step, removing the gourd skin.

2. Once the major portions of the design are designated by the wheel bit, switch to a ball bit, using the pencil grip. Remove the gourd skin from the entire design to be carved. The objective is to simply remove the gourd skin in order to get to the gourd pulp. Don't try to carve all the way to the 1/8th inch depth at this point. Carving should be accomplished in controlled layers.

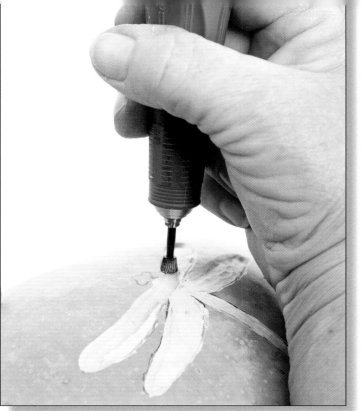

3. Now that the skin is removed and the design visible, insert an inverted cone into the handpiece. Using a pencil grip, with the handpiece held on its end, carefully follow the design line and start removing gourd pulp from inside the carving area. For now, don't try to carve the small corners or tight areas. Using the inverted cone on its end also creates a slightly concave gouge from the edge of the gourd skin to the floor of the carving that helps keep the InLace in place. If the inverted cone is not available, use a medium ball bit.

4. Using a larger ball bit if the design allows, remove the remainder of the gourd pulp from the design. Use short, controlled strokes to remove small amounts of the carving at a time.

25

5. Switch to a smaller ball or engraving bit to clean out corners and tight spots. To get sharp corners, consider the wheel bit or a straight-pointed bit. The floor of the carved area need not be smooth. For very small, tight designs, a diamond dental bit or regular small diamond ball bit can be used to clean the pulp out of these areas.

6a. A flat woodburning tip can also be used to create an undercut in the carved area. Some artists also use the flat woodburning tip to straighten out the edges of the gourd skin surrounding the carved area. This may or may not be desired as it does leave a slightly darker, burned edge.

6. The small engraving bit or any small ball bit can be used to create an undercut in the wall of the carved design, usually at the base of the carving. Hold the handpiece at an angle and carefully drill out a line of gourd pulp. See the illustration for how the undercut should look, if viewed from the side. At this time also use the small ball bit to clean up any rough or uneven edges of the gourd skin that surround the carving.

6b. If the carved design could be viewed from the side, here are two correct ways and one incorrect way that the carving should look. The first correct way is created when the inverted cone is held on end. The cut made is a slight angling of the carving wall. The second correct way is created by a small ball or engraving bit held at an angle so that it removes part of the wall near the floor of the carving. Both these undercuts allow the InLace mixture to flow into them, providing security for the inlay once it is cured. The wrong way, as illustrated, shows the carving simply "scooped" out of the gourd rather than carved.

26

7. Once the pulp has been removed from the carved area, the corners defined, and an undercut created, one final step is to look very closely at the gourd skin that surrounds the carving. It's the old adage, what you see is what you get. Make sure the skin line is not nicked or showing cut marks. Use a piece of micro fine sanding sponge or sandpaper to smooth out any stubborn edges.

8. Remove any debris from the carved area. A toothbrush or paintbrush will work. If debris like fine gourd pulp is left in the carving, especially the corners, it can interfere with the flow of the InLace mixture, causing bubbles that will have to be removed the next day and replaced with fresh inlay material.

9. Now the design has been carved. It should be smooth at the edges, deep enough to hold the inlay, complete with an undercut, free from debris, and ready to accept the inlay material.

Chapter Five

MIXING INLACE

A Word About Gravity

As gourd artists, we fight gravity when working with InLace. The gourd itself is generally curved. The carved areas are, therefore, usually on a curved surface. We have a liquid inlay material. Yet we expect that liquid to mound up and stay where we want it without dripping out of the carved areas. We have ways to help with that although patience and attention are also required.

The end result of placing InLace into a carved area is to have a slightly rounded inlay, rising above the carved area, that we can grind and polish the next day. Here, more is preferable to less. To achieve this nicely rounded inlay, the wet mixture must be worked with up until the time it begins to harden, or between 12 and 20 minutes after the hardener is added. As the wet mixture begins to settle into the undercuts of the carving, more mixture needs to be added. The gourd needs to be moved around during this process, mainly as we try to find that perfect spot where the mixture remains inside the carving without gravity pulling it out the edges. The consistency of the inlay mixture and keeping an eye on how the wet mixture settles are the two most important things in ending up with a nice, rounded inlay.

Multiple carvings can create their own special challenges when it comes to inlaying a liquid inlay material. Using small mixtures and working one area at a time is the best way to tackle multiple carved designs.

Multiple Carved Areas

When doing a simple inlay, say a cabochon, the carved area is typically confining enough so that one InLace mix can be used to fill the entire carving at one time. But what if the design has multiple carved areas, perhaps on three sides of the same gourd, or that the carved design covers the entire side of a gourd, or a rim around the top of the gourd is the carved design? This presents the need for a different approach to placing InLace mixtures into the carvings.

For multiple carvings, concentrate on one controllable area at a time, using smaller mixes. Let one inlay begin the hardening process, and become stable in the carving, before starting to work on another, fresh inlay. To ensure that the color formulas match where needed, simply make a large mix of the color and additives and then divide that mix into several paper cups **before** the hardener is added. Add the hardener to each separate cup when it's time to move on to another area.

For areas such as lines around gourd rims, fill in one short, controllable section at a time. When that section starts to harden, use a fresh batch of InLace and simply push the fresh mix up against the one that is already in place. They will bond without any lines.

Using Premixed and Solid/ Opaque InLace

The ten InLace colors are shown in the front section of this book. These mixtures vary greatly in texture. By texture, this refers to the thickness of the original mix as it comes out of the InLace can. Thickness is important because the final resin mixture needs to be thin enough to flow into small, carved areas yet thick enough to hold itself together as we work to get to the optimal rounded inlay. **The right consistency is that of jam**.

The only InLace mixture that is almost perfect is the color called Lacey. For beginners, Lacey is the best color mixture to learn with, but always be aware that even Lacey may need a little Thicken-it if the carved area is on a very curved spot on the gourd.

Now, in a well ventilated area, get the workstation ready. Assemble paper products, mixing sticks, selected InLace products, screwdriver, hammer, acetone and rags, paper plates, toothpicks, and Q-tips. Open canisters of additives or loosen jar lids. The only item that should remain **closed** is the jar of Thicken-it. Never take a chance that the contents could be spilled. They are light, fluffy, and should not be inhaled. If spilled, use a vacuum to clean up immediately. A mask should be available if Thicken-it is to be added. A mask should also be on hand in case you find the odor of InLace offensive.

Last but not least, have a small notepad handy. Write down the color InLace used, any additives and their amounts (three drops violet dye, two pea sized copper penny dust, etc.), and what carving/gourd the mixture was used in. This way, if there is a problem with the original inlay and more mixture needs to be made 24-hours later, the formula is available. Or perhaps the colors used looks terrific and would look great on a gourd carved sometime in the future. Some wood turners even make color samples of their standard mixtures, inset into the raw wood, for future reference.

1. A freshly opened can of InLace most likely will have a thin layer of it's base liquid sitting on the top of the color mixture. The entire can must be mixed thoroughly, using a wooden mixing stick.

2. Determine how much InLace will be needed to fill the carved area. Judging this will come with experience. Using a wooden mixing stick, place the fresh InLace from the can into the one-ounce paper cup. It's almost impossible to "pour" InLace from the can into the small paper cup. Place the mixing stick on the paper plate when done transferring.

3. Add any colorants such as metallic dust, dye, or granules. Using the end of a fresh mixing stick is the best way to transfer colorants, small amounts at a time, from their original containers to the paper cup. I wipe off this new stick so it can be used again unless it's been used to transfer dye. For dye, I leave the stick on the paper plate in case another drop or two is needed. For mixing the ingredients, I use the original transfer stick. Always close up bottles and packages after using them. Spilled dye is not only expensive, but also truly messy.

4. Determine the thickness of the mixture now that all the colorants have been added. Is it like jam or is it still running freely off the end of the mixing stick? If the mix is not as thick as it should be, add Thicken-it. Be sure your face mask is in place. Carefully open the jar of Thicken-it and, using the end of a clean mixing stick, measure out about a pea sized amount. Deposit that into the paper cup and mix well using the original mixing stick. Keep checking the consistency, adding small amounts with the clean stick, and stirring until all the white flakes are incorporated.

6. Transferring the mixture into the gourd carving comes next. What is used to transfer the mix depends on the size of the carving, but generally start with the mixing stick. Plop (a nice descriptive word for it) some of the mixture into the largest part of the gourd carving. Begin to spread the resin around with the stick. Add more mixture, working from the center outwards to the edges, but not over the edges, of the carving. If the carved design is small, transfer the mix to the carving using a flat-ended toothpick or the cut end of the Q-tip.

5. Once the consistency is judged thick enough, add the InLace Hardener. The amount of drops used will depend on the amount of mix. Judging how much mix is in the cup will come with experience. Even if the original measurement was a half-ounce, adding other ingredients and liquids may have made the mix slightly larger.

This is why there is a range in the ratio of drops of hardener-to-mix chart. Most gourd artists who use InLace have learned to estimate the size of the mix and adjust the hardener accordingly. A drop or two more will usually not effect the mixture. Five or six drops will, especially if the mixture is overly thick. A few drops less than needed and there may not be enough to start the hardening process. This is one of the tricky parts of using InLace — but a few goofs and a few perfect mixes later, it will all make sense. For use with Clear InLace, use the higher number of drops:

*Ratio of InLace Hardener to InLace Mix
*¾ teaspoon InLace=4 to 5 drops hardener
*1 teaspoon InLace=6 to 7 drops hardener
*half-ounce InLace = 10 to 12 drops hardener
*1 ounce InLace=19 to 22 drops hardener

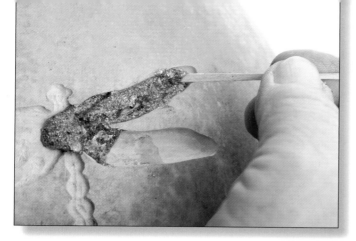

7. For corners or small-carved areas, use a toothpick to drag the mixture into the space. The toothpick-dragging method also helps eliminate air pockets. The angled end of a cut Q-tip also works for pushing the mixture into tight spaces. Plus the cotton end of the Q-tip is very handy for wiping up small drops, or for pushing errant edges of the material back into the carving. I always have a bunch of Q-tips handy because, once used, they should be tossed out.

Keep adding mixture as the InLace settles into the undercuts in the carving. This settling may take a few minutes so watch the resin carefully, holding the gourd in the hands all the time while trying to find that magic level spot. A good way to check whether or not the mix is starting to harden, rather than touching the inlay itself, is to test the mixture left in the mixing cup.

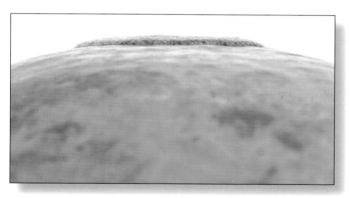

8. The desired result of all this placing, pushing, and adding is to have a nicely rounded inlay by the time the hardening process starts. The accompanying photo shows what that mounding should look like as seen from the side of the gourd. Once the resin is no longer liquid, the gourd can be set upright.

There are two common problems beginners have in determining the "rounding" of an inlay. The first is to make the inlay very high. All this means is that it will take a little longer to grind the inlay down the next day. The second area for concern is allowing dips in the inlay that fall below the gourd skin level.

This is a little more troublesome because this lower area should be carved out of the hardened inlay, and a fresh mixture added to correct the low spot

Now for the hardest part — waiting for the mix to harden. I always wait the full 24-hours. Clean up the workstation, clean off InLace cans with acetone, toss out mixing materials and the paper plate, tighten tops on jars, and close up any opened packages.

Using Clear InLace

Using Clear InLace resin is a little more tricky than using the color mixtures simply because it has absolutely no additives. It **is** the clear base used in other InLace products. Color and texture are, therefore, usually added to Clear InLace. Thicken-it is always added. It takes more time to get the clear formula to the desired jam-like consistency, but there are endless possibilities for tone and texture.

With Clear InLace, the same rules apply as for any InLace resin covered in the previous pages. Approach multiple carved areas by doing small areas at a time, work on keeping the gourd level, and the inlay confined within the carving, and allowing one inlay to start to harden before moving on to another area.

Prepare the work area with the same materials used for pre-mixed or solid/opaque and have everything ready; paper plate, cups, acetone, mixing sticks, etc.

Open the can of Clear. Don't be alarmed at the blue color; the mixture will harden clear.

1. Transfer the Clear InLace into a paper cup using a wooden mixing stick. Please don't try to pour the clear formula out of the can. It will only drip down the edges of the can and make a mess.

2. Unless a clear inlay is desired, InLace dye needs to be added. Open the selected bottle of dye and make sure it is well mixed with a clean wooden stick. To add to the resin, let the color drop off the end of the stick into the mixing cup. Put the stick off to one side on the paper plate in case more color is needed. Return to the original stick and mix well. If the color is what you want, proceed from there. If not, add a few more drops.

3. Because Clear InLace has no additives or color chips, if texture is desired, then stone flakes, nuggets, granules, or metallic dust needs to be added. Transfer small amounts from the end of a clean stick to the paper cup. Mix well after each addition with the original stick.

4. Clear InLace always requires Thicken-it, but before adding it, mix in all the other additives first. When ready to add Thicken-it, put on a face mask. Carefully open the container and use a clean mixing stick to transfer small amounts (pea sized) into the paper cup. Mix well after each addition, using the original transfer stick, until the white flakes have fully incorporated. Keep adding small amounts of Thicken-it until the consistency becomes jam-like.

5. Finally, add the appropriate number of drops of hardener. Use the higher number of drops to mix noted in the Ratio chart.

6. The procedure for transferring Clear InLace into a carved area is the same as any of the color mixtures. Refer to the previous pages for hints on how to control the mixture as it is placed into the carving, how to determine what areas of the carving to do first, mounding the mixture, and the hardening timeframe.

Chapter Six:

GRINDING, SANDING, AND POLISHING

Step 1.
Sanding Drums

The first step in reducing the amount of hardened inlay from the rounded mound to the level of the gourd skin is grinding. The sanding drum is a good choice to accomplish this. In selecting sanding drums and other sanding materials, the "grit" needs to be understood. Grit refers to the coarseness of the sanding material. Low numbered grits are rougher. As the numbers go higher, the grit becomes finer. To reduce a resin inlay, I typically start with a grit in the 80 to 120 range.

A respirator or face mask is essential throughout the entire grinding to polishing process. Insert a mandrel and sanding drum into the rotary tool. Using **low** speed, and keeping the curved side of the sanding drum level with the gourd skin, begin to grind the inlay. Short, even sideways strokes are preferable to holding the drum in one place. Try to not angle the sanding drum. This will cause gouges and may reduce the inlay to below gourd skin level, or may nick the carving edges. See the two photos that show the right

and wrong ways to angle the handpiece. The objective of this first sanding process is to reduce the resin inlay to just **above** gourd skin level.

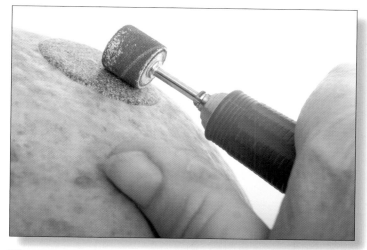

The correct angle to use when first reducing a hardened inlay with a coarse sanding drum is to hold the drum flat against the inlay.

The angle of the sanding drum, shown here, will cause gouges in the inlay as well as the potential for nicking the edge of the gourd skin.

Step 2.
Sanding Sponges and Sandpaper

Following the initial reduction of the inlay, hand-sanding is required to bring the inlay to gourd skin level. I use sanding sponges, starting with 120 grit and ending with 320. Sandpaper and sanding blocks may also be used. This hand-sanding process takes time, so **don't** rush it.

To determine if the inlay has been reduced sufficiently, close your eyes and run your fingertips over the inlay and the surrounding gourd. The fingertips should "slide" right over the inlay. If high spots or bumps and dips are felt, continue hand-sanding. Holding the gourd up to a good light source helps show imperfections, too.

Rotary sanders can be used in place of hand-sanding. Sanding discs in the 400 to 1200 grit range can create a beautiful finish with little damage to the gourd skin. Lower grits, however, used on a rotary must be used with caution.

Both the buffing and polishing compound can be applied directly to the inlay rather than to the felt or muslin wheel.

To reduce the inlay to gourd skin level, hand-sanding the inlay can be accomplished with any type of sanding sponge, block, or sandpaper ranging from fine to micro fine.

Step 3.
Final Buffing and Polishing

Once the resin inlay has been reduced to gourd skin level with hand-sanding, insert a mandrel with a felt or muslin wheel into the rotary tool. Apply the brown InLace buffing compound **directly** onto the inlay. Turn the rotary tool on **low** speed, and using light touches with the felt wheel, work the compound into the inlay. Be sure the face mask or respirator is still being worn. Bits of the compound will spin off the inlay. The In-Lace buffing compound is designed to remove slight scratches left by the sanding process.

Lastly, apply the white polishing compound directly onto the inlay and use the same technique as for the buffing compound; low speed and light touches. I don't bother to change the felt wheel between the compounds unless the felt had become clogged.

After the polishing, turn the inlay to the light or sunlight. The white compound not only shines the inlay, but also highlights any dips or bumps that might have been missed. Return to hand-sanding, followed by the brown compound, etc. Repeat as necessary.

A handy way to remember which compound comes first, buffing or polishing, simply remember the alphabet. "B" for brown and buffing come before "W" for white or "P" for polishing.

Using the felt or muslin wheel on LOW speed and with a light touch will help the compounds do their job.

Add a protective coat of varnish or acrylic finish to the inlay if further work is to be done on the gourd, such as dyes, stains, or paints. The protective coat makes it easier to remove any errant color that might get on the inlay.

As a final protective coat for the entire gourd, any spray or brush-on finish can go right over the inlay. However, if wax is used, I tend to avoid putting the wax over the InLace. The inlay is already shiny from the first protective coating and wax may dull the finish.

A coat of varnish or polyurethane is added to the completed inlay—to protect it from colorants that may be used when finishing the gourd.

Chapter Seven

TROUBLESHOOTING
& Other Questions

Q. My InLace mixture set up before I finished placing it into the carving. What happened and what can I do?

A. There are several explanations for this. One, there were too many additives to the mixture and it was beyond the correct consistency before the activator was added. Never go beyond 50/50 ratio of additives to resin. The answer is to constantly check consistency. If the mixture becomes too thick, a few drops of acetone might help. Or just leave the mixture in the paper cup, let it cure and create a cabochon out of it. Move on to a fresh mix.

Two, too much hardener was added; that will cause the mixture to set up quickly. Answer, carefully count the drops of hardener as they are added to the mixture and that the hardener is the last thing added.

And three, too much time was taken insetting the mixture. The window available to work with InLace is usually between 12 and 20 minutes, depending on the mixture. If the area is so large that you didn't have time to complete the inlay, just mix up a fresh batch using the same formula and continue insetting. The two mixtures will blend together without leaving a line.

Q. My inlay has a bubble in it after it hardened. What should I do?

A. Bubbles are caused in several ways. First, there might have been gourd pulp dust left in the carving. Be sure to thoroughly clean the carving with a brush before insetting the inlay. Second, when insetting the inlay mixture, you didn't use toothpicks or ends of Q-tips to drag the mixture into corners and tight areas. Using the toothpick helps remove air bubbles.

To fix bubbles or low spots after the inlay has cured, grind out the offending area using a small ball bit, create a mix to match what is in the inlay, and inset the fresh mix. When hardened, you will need to grind, sand, and buff/polish the new area.

Q. My inlay still wasn't set after 24-hours. What can I do?

A. Basically, you should wipe out the wet inlay with a rag and acetone, and start over. Humidity and temperature might have some effect on curing, but if the inlay is still very soft and runny, wipe it out. The initial error may have been additives to mix ratio or hardener-to-mix ratio. Carefully estimate the amount of mix before the hardener is added. Remember, if textures/colors like stone flakes, dye, or granules are added, the original half-ounce might be closer to three-quarters; therefore, the number of drops of hardener is adjusted.

Q. The areas around my inlay seem rough and uneven. What happened?

A. The final step before mixing and insetting the inlay is to "run the eye" around the edges of the carving. If you can see nicks or uneven lines, that is what will show once the inlay is hardened. Sanding sponges, lightly applied as the final step before mixing InLace, will help. Or carefully use a small ball bit to even out the gourd skin line.

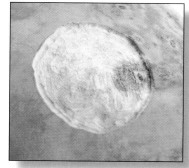

The edges of this carving are rough and uneven, and the gourd skin is gouged. The inlay, therefore, will not be smooth along it's edges.

An engraving bit or small ball bit can be used to remove a bubble or troublesome area from a hardened inlay, which is then filled with a fresh InLace mixture.

Q. When I re-opened my can of InLace, there were crystals in the mix and it seems very thick. What can I do?

A. The shelf life for InLace is approximately one year if stored in a controlled environment. Be sure your supplies are kept at or below 72 degrees. If the crystals are only on the can rim, this might be caused by not closing the lid tightly with a hammer or from not cleaning the can rim with acetone before closing. If the crystals and thickness are in the mixture itself, then air might have leaked into the can or it might be beyond the shelf life. Crystals indicate that the hardening properties of InLace have been compromised. When in doubt, test the mixture on a gourd scrap, not your good carving. If the mixture does not harden, toss the can of InLace out.

Q. I broke through to the inside of the gourd when carving. Can it be fixed?

A. Yes. There are several products on the market to help when a carving breaks through to the inside of the gourd. Any of the wood putty products, like QuikWood® or Speedybond®, can be used to patch the hole, usually from the inside of the gourd. For tiny holes or weak spots, use either of the wood putty products or Terra Bella's Wood Texture and Filler® from either the inside or outside of the gourd. Let the patches dry before resuming. And remember, the floor of the carving doesn't need to be smooth so there is no need to sand down or reduce the patch.

Breaking through the gourd to the inside can happen while carving. Just patch from the inside using any formula of wood-crafting putty, like QuikWood or Speedybond. Tiny holes can be patched from either side with the Terra Bella Wood Filler.

Q. How many inlays can I make from a can of InLace?

A. That will depend on the size of the inlays. Basically there is enough mixture in two ounces to do a 15-foot by 1/8 inch by 1/8-inch inlay. Or, if using a half-ounce for each inlay, there are eight inlays available in a four-ounce can. This isn't an absolute answer because adding textures can extend the original measurement.

Q. I didn't use all my mix for the inlay. What can I do with the leftovers?

A. Leftover mixes can be left in the bottom of the one-ounce paper cup and popped out when hardened, ground, and polished to use as a cabochon. Or small amounts of the wet mixture can be dropped onto the paper plate and used the same way.

Q. When I was insetting the inlay material, it ran all over the place and I couldn't control it. What can I do?

A. If the inlay mix is uncontrollable because of incorrect consistency or because you've tried to insert the material in multiple areas on a curve and gravity is fighting you, I would wet a rag with acetone and quickly wipe the entire inlay out. Then start over. Make a fresh mix, adjust the consistency with Thicken-it, and reapply. Leave the first mixture in the paper cup, let it harden, and then use it as a cabochon.

If an InLace mixture is too thin, e.g. not the texture of jam, it can flow right out the sides of the carving.

Q. My can of Clear InLace is blue, not "clear." Is this wrong?

A. Clear InLace is slightly blue in color, but it does dry clear.

Q. I don't want to invest a lot of money right now on equipment and InLace. Are there any options?

A. Yes. There is a Starter Kit that I developed, offered by Turtle Feathers. The kit consists of your choice of a four-ounce can of InLace color mixture (or eight-ounces of Clear), hardener, sticks, paper cups, one-ounce sizes of buffing and polishing compound, one-ounce of Thicken-it, a small amount of metallic dust, Proxxon sanding drums and mandrel, Proxxon felt wheels and mandrel, and the manufacturer's warnings and precautions. Also included are Q-tips, toothpicks, and directions written in "gourd" language. All you need besides this kit is a gourd, a rotary tool of some type, and a few bits. It's a good way to try InLace to see if it's a product you like without a lot of running around to find specific tools and equipment. A good choice of color mixture for beginners is Lacey as it is almost always the correct consistency for inlays.

Q. When sanding, I removed some of the skin surrounding the inlay. What can I do to repair this?

A. For minor skin removal, a little Gilders Paste rubbed in with a Q-tip, or a diluted rust toned alcohol ink applied in light layers, might help. Build up color gradually until the mark is as close as possible to the original skin tone. Or woodburn around the design. This is also helpful if nicks are taken out of the skin during the grinding process.

For major skin removal that can't be stained to your satisfaction, there are several things you can do. One, use acrylic paint around the inlay. Two, woodburning around the inlay may help the situation. Three, consider carving around the inlay.

Repairing a blemish in the gourd skin around an inlay can be accomplished with several light applications of Gilders Paste, or a very diluted dye or ink solution.

Q. My carved design runs all around the side of my gourd. Can I do the inlay all at one time?

A. No. With multiple carved inlays, or carvings that take up a lot of gourd surface or run around the rim, using several smaller mixtures is best. The same will run true if a specific color mixture is to be used in two areas of the gourd but are separated by a curve in the gourd. Do them one at a time, letting the first mixture reach a stage where the gourd can be placed upright without the inlay running out, and then mixing a fresh, small batch to do another inlay

area, etc. Just take care to not bump the previous inlays. It takes several hours before the inlay is hard enough to take a direct hit.

Where the additional mixtures meet, as in a gourd rim, they will blend without leaving a line as long as they are comprised of the same formula. A good idea for future reference in working with inlays is to write down the formulas used to create the color mixture, and the inlay/carved design for which the resin inlay was used.

Q. I used a foam bowl to hold the resin and it dissolved. How come?

A. InLace resins are acetone based. Acetone will eat through foam or plastic cups. Use paper cups to hold resin mixtures. The exception to this is using a plastic bag to mix and distribute resins in small, intricate areas. Read the article by A. B. Amis in the Artists' Perspectives section for further information.

Q. Can I add real stone or metal filings to InLace?

A. People often ask if components other than those that come in the product line can be added to InLace. My answer is always the same. I don't know because I find all the ingredients I want right in the InLace family. I haven't felt any need to experiment, yet. If you do wish to experiment, test mixes on gourd scraps. Don't attempt on a good, carved design. In addition, real stone requires a coarser grit and higher speed to grind it down so this can lead to gouging and overheating of the resin.

Q. While I was polishing with my felt wheel and rotary tool, my inlay got sticky. What happened?

A. Most likely, you were using a fast speed on the rotary tool. When buffing and polishing, use low speed and a very light touch.

Q. I have carved my design to be inlayed. Can I stain and paint my gourd before I do the InLace?

A. It is always best to do the coloring of the gourd after the inlay has been ground, sanded, and a protective coat of varnish or polyurethane placed on the InLace. There are several reasons for doing it this way. One, if you have to wipe off any errant spills of InLace, there is a chance of also wiping off the colorant on the gourd itself. And two, there is the possibility of removing the paint/stain from around the inlay during the grinding/sanding process. As most gourd artists will tell you, matching and patching of any gourd colorant is not the easiest thing to accomplish.

The following articles, written by gourd artisans and a wood turner, are provided to give more insight and understanding of resin inlays. Several artisans offer their experiences in teaching and working with InLace while others provide a how-to for specific projects. More of their work plus additional artists' photographs can be found in the Gallery.

♥♥♥♥♥♥

Bonnie Gibson: "Comparison of Three Inlay Resins"

Inlaying stone and resin is a very tedious and laborious process. Don't try this if you get frustrated easily or like to finish projects fast!

So far, I have tried three different products for inlaying crushed stone/resin mixtures. There are many other products yet to try, but here are the results I obtained with these particular three.

System Three Resin®

After trying their two-part liquid product, I'd have to say that the System Three resin just is not something that would work well for gourd inlay. It is very thin and almost impossible to use on a curved surface such as a gourd. I'm sure it would be great on level surfaces such as tabletops. If you wait until it starts to get thick enough to actually stay where you put it on a curved surface, it sets almost immediately at that point and you can't work it into the area. I had to build up some dams with tape to hold the material in place, and even then I had to go back and reapply the resin a second time to replace areas where it had run out. I mixed this with some synthetic lapis stone granules, blue opalescent dye, and a few metallic flakes.

Epoxy 330®

A substance I had good luck with was Epoxy 330, manufactured by Hughes Associates of Wayzata, Minnesota. (Where I grew up!!) It is sold for use in jewelry inlay applications and doesn't yellow over time like some other epoxies. It comes packaged in two tubes. You mix equal parts from each tube. I mixed some crushed white synthetic stone granules and mica flakes into the mixture. I found this was easy to use, relatively inexpensive, and sets quickly. This epoxy had a much thicker consistency than the System Three and mostly stayed where it was applied. You will need to paint the gourd underneath the inlaid area, or add dye to the epoxy. I tried using it without doing either of these things and found that the epoxy looked yellow because it picked up the underlying color of the gourd.

Examples of a zigzag design can be seen on Bonnie's bowl titled the Parrot. *Photography and copyright ® by Everett Gibson.*

InLace

InLace is a product generally sold to woodworkers for decorative filling of gaps in burl wood bowls, etc. It works well for them as well as gourd artists because it comes premixed in various formulas and colors, and is thick enough to stay where you place it on a curved surface. While this product is somewhat pricey, a little goes a long way. One can of InLace will do many gourd projects. InLace tends to be the most strong smelling of the three mixtures and wearing a respirator while using it is recommended.

Author's Note: Visit Bonnie's web site, www.arizona-gourds.com, for more tutorials as well as tools and equipment for gourd art.

♥♥♥♥♥♥

Gary Devine: "Power Carving InLace"

Power carving InLace is a fairly simple technique that can be achieved by using only a limited number of carving bits or dental burs, your imagination in patterning, care, and a lot of patience. InLace carving may be used anywhere on a gourd project, but I find it very useful in borders, dividing designs, or covering the transition from one gourd piece to another when joining multiple pieces.

Materials

The tools required to carve on a cured resin inlay include a power carving tool (preferably with a flexi-shaft and stand), InLace, a small drum attachment with both medium and fine grits, and an assortment of carving burs, including carbide and diamond (coarse 1/16" football and needle). Dental burs of a high quality are recommended. Lesser expensive ones will heat up and be destroyed. Never use diamond burs for the first stage of carving InLace. Diamond burs are used for soft material carving only.

Preparing a Gourd Medallion

On a fairly thick piece of gourd, measure out an 8.5 cm diameter and draw a circle. Cut out the piece and then mark another circle within the medallion, which is 6 cm in diameter. Use an inverted V cutting bit to outline the inside of the circle and then a ball cutter or structured tooth bit to remove the rest of the inside space (eye protection is advised).

Prepare the InLace of your choice by following the directions and pour it into the cut out portion. Leave a slight overlap onto the bordering area and mound it a bit. Let it dry for a day.

Carving the Inlay

1. Reducing the Inlay

Put on a respirator or dust mask. Use the drum sander to smooth out the InLace surface so that you

Vase, handle detail.

barely expose the gourd border. Shape it so that it is somewhat convex in the middle. You'll need a gentle hand for this. Repairs can be made, but they are time consuming. Lastly, carve or sand down the InLace so that it melds smoothly into the gourd border. A smooth sanding stone is helpful in order to avoid damaging the gourd surface.

2. Placing a design on the Medallion

Now it's time to begin the design. You may either draw directly on the InLace with a graphite pencil or trace it on the surface using transfer paper. A red pen helps tell you what you've already traced. Be sure the darker surface of the transfer paper is down.

Because the carving process is a very dusty one, your drawing will become immediately obscured. As a result, you'll have to keep clearing away the dust, which in turn will probably rub out your design. To avoid this, you must first go over your design lines with a very fine, permanent, black marker.

3. The first step in carving with this technique is to outline all of the design with the football-shaped dental bur. Try to maintain a uniform depth in the cuts to a depth approximately equal to the width of the bit. A smooth pulling motion away from the body should facilitate this. Use a medium to medium-high speed with the Dremel or other rotary tool.

4. After the entire design is outlined, clear out the background with the same bur. Then, use the needle-shaped diamond bur to put in fine detail or clean up any blurry lines in the design.

5. Apply a clear finish with a wide brush that you have loaded **sparingly**. This dry brush technique is achieved by dragging the side of the brush lightly across the higher areas of the design. The background is left unfinished so that it contrasts with the foreground. As an alternative to the dry brush technique, you may like to apply a very thin wash of white paint to the carving and then wipe off the access. Then, apply a sealer.

Hint: To help alleviate the dust problem, I hold the gourd in my lap and the nozzle to a vacuum in my non-carving hand.

Dental bits can be obtained from dental supply houses or online from various suppliers that sell tools and equipment.

♥♥♥♥♥♥

A. B. Amis: "How **NOT** to Teach an InLace Class"

Probably like lots of other folks, I "discovered" InLace back around 2003 when Turtle Feathers first began bringing it around to gourd shows. And being more of an artisan than artist, my early efforts were just simple geometric projects like those shown here.

The tall vase was my first project, and my attempts at filling the angular cutouts with InLace material using just the wooden spatulas supplied with the kits were sort of hit and miss, leaving lots of messy material to be filed and sanded off in some areas and leaving voids that had to be re-filled later in others.

Using hand tools and sandpaper (very tedious work), I was able to get the InLace down *almost* flush without having marred the adjacent gourd surfaces. But then when I finally had to resort to using a vibratory sander for the final sanding, I discovered that it really didn't matter all that much if I actually touched the gourd surface as long as I was using very fine grit paper, like 400 grit. In fact, I discovered later that I could even achieve a pleasing "halo" effect around the InLace by intentionally lightly sanding (again with very fine grit paper) the surrounding area, as demonstrated in the darker piece with the InLace titled "Jewel."

By removing the gourd skin from around the inlay, a halo design is created.

Wishing for a neater way of placing InLace material in cutouts, I discovered that I could use small plastic baggies, first placing the raw InLace material in the bag, adding a few drops (determined by experimentation) of accelerator, mixing by squishing the bag for a few seconds, and then cutting off one corner and squeezing the InLace out in much the same way as a cake decorator might do. This technique allowed me to progress on to designs involving narrower cutouts (which I made mostly using gouges, since carving is my "thing").

Emboldened by my successes, I agreed to teach an InLace project at our local gourd patch, breaking the class into two parts. In the first part students would trace a simple design (like a bear with the heart line), carve it out using thin veiner gouges, and then fill the cutouts with InLace using the little baggie technique. Then in the second session, after the InLace had hardened, students would finish the project. The tracing and carving part went just fine inside our library meeting room, after which we moved outside to a park bench so as to not stink up the whole library with InLace's very pungent chemical smell.

After explaining the intended process, I issued baggies and began filling the bags and dropping in the accelerator for the dozen students, all anxiously waving their baggies at me. This preparation process turned out to take far longer than I had expected. By the time I had finished, InLace was everywhere except where it was supposed to be. It was on fingers and Kleenex tissues where some students had tried to wipe off overfills, even on one lady's purse that she'd let fall over onto her otherwise neatly-done piece. (Luckily I'd brought a can of acetone and a roll of paper towels.) And because I'd been too occupied with filling baggies, I failed to

An example of a simple yet effective rim design with InLace.

notice that the students had overfilled their cutouts, misunderstanding the term "slightly mounded." They also enthusiastically probed their inlays for air bubbles with a toothpick and some students ended up having to add more InLace at the next meeting and not finish sanding and polishing until a third session. *Live and learn!* The next time I was asked about teaching an InLace class, I opted just to do a demo instead!

*Author's Note: This technique for using a baggie to hold InLace, cutting off the edge, and then squeezing the inlay material out into small areas does work. The trick is to cut off only a **tiny** corner of the bag to help control the flow. Also be sure to close the top of the bag or the InLace will bubble up and over. Thanks to A. B. for coming up with this creative way to handle InLace.*

♥♥♥♥♥♥♥

Randall Eckley: "Inlaid Gourd Bowl"

Day One

1. Select a gourd that sits well and/or sand the bottom flat. I force the bottom against a five-inch rotating bench sander — a good investment at $30-$50 for all sorts of jobs.

2. Use a stationary pencil touching the gourd surface and turn the gourd to mark cut line for removing the gourd top.

3. Carefully cut top off with hand-held jig saw — Microlux®, Proxxon®, Craftsman, etc. Remember, this cut will be the gourd's rim and needs to be horizontal with the surface on which it will sit.

4. Remove inside pulp and seeds. Sand inside surface roughly with coarse 60-grit sandpaper. Dress the inner aspect of the rim with 150, then 220-grit sandpaper.

5. Using five-minute epoxy, mix and distribute a generous amount to all inner surfaces of the gourd. There are three reasons to do this. One, this strengthens the walls; two, assures that any dye applied to interior cannot penetrate to the surface; and three, helps you to avoid puncturing the gourd while working the surface.

6. Mark the position of the channel that you want to "rout." Very even and parallel lines are important.

Important: Use safety glasses and a good-quality dust mask when carving.

7. A bright light, patience and practice are needed from here on. You will eventually be able to excavate (rout) perfectly straight channels as you get comfortable with using a rotary tool and a bur. MY FIRST INLAY WAS VERY UNEVEN.

8. Move the gourd surface into the spinning bur and turn the gourd in the left hand while securing the rotary tool in the right hand. I do this seated with halogen light above. Working on your lap, set the rotary tool to the 'correct' speed. You will learn (through

practice) what the right speed is for your project. Are you left-handed? Then hold the project in your right hand, grinder in the left hand and the strong light source over your left shoulder.

9. Rotation speed needs to be A) fast enough to cut the surface and B) slow enough to give you control. Excessive rpm's will result in the cutter skipping and gouging where you don't want it to go.

10. The goal now is to make channels with walls **perpendicular** to the surface. The reason? The design will be wavy and irregular if walls are not perpendicular to the surface as the design is ground/sanded. Keeping the cutting bur at a right angle to the surface is how this is accomplished.

The cuts should be deep enough to accept a generous amount of inlay resin, but not deep enough to puncture the interior of the bowl. Occasional slips in depth are not a problem, just try to avoid piercing through excessively. We are weakening the gourd's strength and durability by all of this cutting, BUT when the design is filled with resin and hardened, it will be stronger and more durable than before. Resin does not "dry," it hardens.

11. Once that you have defined the perimeter of the design, cut the gourd surface away from inside the lines. Again, patience is required. Don't hurry this part. If the tool gets away from you, you will put nicks and notches into your carefully prepared vertical perimeter

A double rim design is a decorative way to treat a gourd bowl.

walls. By now you have gourd dust all over you and your work area. Clean it up.

12. Now the inlay resin! Remove all dust from the project by blowing or brushing. I use canned air and a horse hair shoe brush.

13. With electrician's tape, cover the surface of the gourd skin surrounding the design. This keeps the excess liquid resin from attaching to too much of the surface where it is not wanted. Once you grind to the

tape surface, tape can be removed, leaving a clean surface. This saves on sanding time and effort the next day.

Now, make sure that your work area is ventilated — this is the stinky part.

14. Mix the resin (I use polyurethane disposable gloves). Open the resin can and stir well. Transfer ½ to 1 ounce into a one-ounce paper cup. I use 48 drops of hardener per ounce and stir well for 60 seconds. Try to avoid stirring in air bubbles. Set a timer for four minutes. Four minutes from now will be GO TIME.

15. Make sure all gourd surfaces are dry and prepare a place that your project can drip e.g., a piece of cardboard. At the four-minute mark, right after the timer goes off, the liquid InLace is 'cooking' but still very fluid. This is good. Four more minutes from go-time and it will be too late as the resin will be gel and unsuitable to transfer. Working quickly, start applying the InLace into the design. Keep pushing the flow back to the design (where you want it) with the wooden stick *and* gravity. Rotate the piece to facilitate gravity pull. The channels need to be completely filled and then some. Too much is fine and too little is not. Work efficiently, so as not to waste product. Multiple small batches are better than too much that cannot be controlled. Tip: inlay resin can be added at any point to fix air bubbles.

16. Once that you are satisfied that all of your design is full of resin and the mixture has stopped moving, it's time to put it away for 12 hours and clean up the mess that you have made. The piece should be left to completely harden at room temperature. Don't place your project near a heat source. It will be sticky for a few hours but just leave it alone. It needs to harden, not dry. Once the hardening has progressed for one to two hours you can stop venting the area. InLace resin will be hard as a rock in 10 to 12 hours. Acetone is the perfect solvent for hands, drips and cleaning surfaces.

Day Two

17. With a rotary tool (I prefer Dremel) and *coarse* sanding drum, CAREFULLY grind off the excess In-Lace until you are close to the gourd surface. Switch to the *fine* sanding drum and carefully (with a light touch) move closer to the surface. The point here is to leave the InLace design as flush to the surface as possible without gouging the surface too much. This requires oblique light and a gentle sweeping back and forth with the rotating sandpaper drum. Use a rag wetted with acetone to remove the electrician's tape residue before step 18.

18. Once you have the fine grinding done, it is time to move on to hand-sanding. Oblique lighting is your friend here. It shows you the hills and valleys of the surface so you know where to sand. I start with 100-grit paper. I have found that if you back the sand-

paper with duct tape, it is easier to use, does a better job and lasts longer. Mark the back with grit number for easy reference.

19. Depending on the project, I use any (or all) of the following sandpapers. Start with 60 grit, followed by 100, 150, 180, 220, 320 and 400, or from medium coarse to very fine.

Try to graze over 'valleys' and reduce 'hills' by working on the area in all directions to blend with the surface 'terrain.' I have tried to spot sand just the bumps and it doesn't work. Always sand the **area** to maintain the curve of the gourd surface. You're finished with sanding when your project passes the "Braille Test." This is when you close your eyes and let your fingers brush over the gourd skin and the inlay. There should be little or no difference. Sanding too much or too little can ruin your project. Knowing when to stop is learned by experience.

20. Once the inlay is smooth and ready to finish, fashion a holder for the gourd from wire clothes hangers or stiff wire. This wire device touches only the inside surface of the gourd. Now for the finishing, which usually takes two or three coats. The finish can be acrylic, which dries quickly, or spar polyurethane, which takes days to dry. I always prefer the latter. Use either gloss or semi-gloss. The finish coat will enhance the surfaces of the project and cover slight imperfections.

Finish Coat Tips

I hurry the spar urethane by hanging the gourd in a 170 degree oven for one to one-and-half hours between coats. An "S" hook over an upper heating element is your hanging point. These hooks can be left in the oven as they don't interfere with the oven's real duty. Drips can be sanded flush between coats so long as the finish is truly dry.

Weight can be added by adding BB shot to the bottom of gourd, submerged in freshly mixed five-minute epoxy. If you use the BB shot, once the epoxy has cured, paint the bowl black and line the interior floor with black leather to finish the piece. This makes the interior of your bowl 'disappear' optically.

Once the outside surface is how you want it, you can use paste wax and a silk cloth to 'warm' the finish a little. Krylon Acrylic Spray is good and dries quickly. Minwax Helmsman Spar Urethane spray is best and is waterproof.

Author's Note: The reader might notice that Randy has used twice the amount of hardener-to-mixture than the suggested ratio. Randy is an experienced gourd artisan who has developed a system that works for him. By setting the timer, he can work within an eight-minute timeframe. And by experience, he can "feel" the mixture, when it is liquid and when it passes beyond that point. For those inexperienced in InLace, I suggest you follow the guidelines as outlined in Chapter 5.

♥♥♥♥♥♥

Gloria Crane: "It's not Intimidating, it's Only InLace"

Being new to gourd art, in 2004 I was introduced to a whole new dimension in art. There were so many mediums that could be incorporated into what was seen as a dirty, moldy vegetable. One of the mediums was this resin substance that was being used that looked amazing on gourds. I was intrigued by it and how it was used. I found it to be a beautiful enhancement to the artwork that it had so delicately been inlaid into.

I can remember going into several of the vendors booths at the Welburn Gourd Festival and looking at the boxes of InLace kits for sale. I was new to gourd art and wanted to try everything, but Inlace intimidated me and I wasn't willing to step out of my safe little box and try it on my own. I can even remember picking up a couple of boxes, after laboring over the decision of which colors to choose, before taking that walk up to the register to actually make a purchase. Then I turned around and put those kits right back on the shelf. "I can't do that. It looks too hard and it's way out of my league," I told myself. "That's for those professional gourd artists who know what they're doing."

I left that day without my InLace, but it still haunted me. "How is it done? How do they get it so smooth and even with the gourd? How is it polished? When will my skills be good enough that I too can try it on a gourd?" Well, as luck would have it, it wasn't too much longer and I found a class being taught by none other than Bonnie Gibson. And the class wasn't too far from my home, so I promptly signed up. I was going to learn how to do something the gourd artists do.

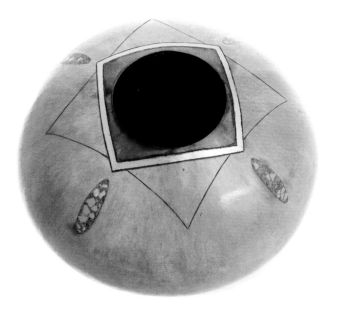

Four tear drops create an eye-catching design on this gourd bowl.

I packed up my Dremel, dust mask and carving burs and headed off to face my fears. I arrived early that day and took a seat at the front of the class, as close to the expert as possible, so I wouldn't miss anything. I hung on every word Bonnie spoke and was the first one out of my seat whenever she would do a demonstration. I learned how to mix the resin and use nuggets and metallic dusts. I learned that 'scary' technique that day and went home thinking how silly I was to not have the confidence in myself to try it on my own. "Now that was much easier than I had ever imagined it would be."

That was an experience with my lack of confidence that I love sharing with my own students now, four years later. I can relate to their fear and intimidation and love to watch as they transform their blank canvases into lovely pieces of art with their beautiful InLace enhancement. You don't have to do fancy or intricate designs that are acquired over time and with a lot of carving experience. Just a simple round or oval design will do, and with a little paste wax to polish it up, your InLace will look like a beautiful inlaid stone.

Step out of your box and don't be intimidated. It's only InLace.

♥♥♥♥♥♥♥

Fonda Haddad: "Gourd Shard Jewelry"

Shards of gourds make an excellent media for InLace gourd jewelry. The gourd surface with its "carveability" and rich patina responds well for jewelry. Any piece that is going to be inlayed needs to be relatively flat and at least 3/8 to 5/8 inch thick without flaws or weak areas. That is not to say they shouldn't have interesting patterns that can be used in the jewelry design but no weak structure areas.

Jewelry from gourd shards over whole gourds have the advantage of letting you know the thickness of the gourd so that one can determine how deep to make the pocket to hold the InLace. Also, it is a wonderful way to use the scrapes from other projects. Gourd shards are strong but light. Earrings, pendants and necklaces may be large but are not heavy.

Because of the wood-like surface, many natural elements and techniques may be incorporated with the InLace, such as woodburning and using paints and stains. Another great thing about jewelry is that it is small, perfect for those little bits of InLace left over from larger projects. Usually I have several pieces of gourd prepared so that when I do a large project and have left over InLace, I can utilize the mixture instantly into the shards. Those shards are then finished into sets of jewelry. You do need to have preplanned sets, carved out to be ready to use.

The nature of InLace techniques is to plan a design and transfer it to the gourd piece by drawing or

Gourd shards can be turned into beautiful jewelry with a little imagination and some InLace.

tracing. I generally woodburn the design even though with grinding and buffing the InLace, the design may have to be reworked. InLace needs to be about one-eights to three-eights deep and should not be to close to the edge of the piece in order not to weaken the jewelry. As with all InLace you need to have a straight line down on the edges of your design and a nice well or carving to capture the compound, creating a slight mounding of the mixture. Because jewelry is small I often encase the InLace in a small plastic bag with the corner tip clipped so that I can place it in the space, like putting icing on a cake.

In order to grind and polish the piece I hold it with needle nose pliers. After it is completely ground and polished, you are ready to do the finishing. Depending on the thickness of the gourd shard and design, re-woodburn and add additional design elements, then seal the shard with clear acrylic or natural shoe polish. If I am going to paint or stain the outside of the design, I choose a color that will bring out the InLace, and the design. Reminder: Always clean and sand the backs of the jewelry. If I need to add a pin finding, I try to leave the attachment spot a little higher than the surrounding areas. The backs can be painted, covered with leather, or woodburned, always keeping in mind that the back is important, but not as much as the front.

Because of the naturalness of gourd pieces, many materials work well to transfer the gourd shard into jewelry including leather, waxed linen, or wire. Keep the materials simple so that they bring out the design rather than distract. Let the InLace design be the focal point. Since the shard is thick you will be able to attach cording, insert screw eyes or earring wires directly into the gourd without fear of the gourd breaking. Beads are a natural embellishment and can continue your theme and enhance your design. The shard may be encased or a fringe added to the bottom.

♥♥♥♥♥♥♥

Bob Malik: "Inlay for Wood Turning"

The use of decorative inlays in wood turning can be most exciting and rewarding. It can add a dimension of texture and color to enhance the natural beauty of the wood. In my studio I use a variety of techniques to decorate my turnings. Inlay of stone-like material, metallic filings and powders, fine sawdust, inset beads, inset stone, along with painting with aniline dyes. I started experimenting with inlay several years ago and I have not looked back.

Wood turning on a lathe allows for techniques that are much different than decorating gourds in many ways. In woodturning we create a perfectly round vessel and we can use the lathe in a spinning and non-spinning mode. Furthermore an indexing system on most lathes allows the artist to establish evenly divided points on the vessel. The use of these tools lends themselves perfectly to adding inlays to your work.

In my studio I work primarily with wet logs that were harvested at historic sites. In wet turning you can complete turning a vessel in one session with a finish that is smooth and clean. The piece will then have to be slow dried. During the drying process some woods will warp slightly and crack. This being said, provisions for inlay must be planned for and implemented at the initial turning while the vessel is still round. In dry woodturning it is not as critical to provide grooves for inlays at the initial turning.

Plan out in advance what the finished piece will be before you do the turning. I find a sketch of the final design is very helpful. As you do the turning, flesh out the final shape. Arrive at a vessel thickness

The two turned wooden bowls shown here are examples of inlays using InLace nuggets.
Photography and copyright ® by Burt Danielson.

Bob uses a lathe to provide the final buffing on his goblet.
Photography and copyright ® by Burt Danielson.

that will allow for the removal of material for your inlay and still be strong and sound. Do all your final smoothing and sanding.

Now you are ready to start your inlay designs. While the work is spinning, make a pencil mark of the position and thickness of your inlay. Next use your parting tool to create a groove or dado to a depth of 1/16 to 1/8 of an inch. Taking special care that the outside edges are smooth and clean. This is the basic groove for a horizontal stripe of inlay. You can add more interest by adding additional stripes along the vessel. You can now add circles to intersect the line. With the lathe off, setup a drill guide on your tool rest holder, set to a height equal to half of the lathes capacity. That is on a 12-inch lathe the height will be six inches, on a 14-inch lathe the height will be seven inches. With the index system locked in at a starting point, drill a circle with a forstner bit to depth equal to the depth of your inlay groove. Then count off equal indents on the index system for the position of the next circle.

Combinations of horizontal stripes and holes of varying sizes can yield many design variations. You can use a wire burner on the spinning piece to create space for painting with aniline dyes.

Free-hand designs can be done by gouging out a groove with a Dremel tool or carving with wood chisels. Dry the piece in your normal manner before proceeding to the inlay.

I use a variety of materials for inlay from coffee grounds to metal filings and powders. InLace nuggets and granules from Turtle Feathers offer a myriad of colors and textures to satisfy any taste. Always dry-mix in a separate container the blend you intend to use, making sure you will have enough of a mix to complete the inlay on the piece. Not mixing enough material will result in a miss matching of the final inlay. Clamp your work on the non-spinning lathe to hold the piece while you do the inlay. Fill in the grooves using the same mixing techniques as described for

gourds. Make sure the groove is clean and dry and only work small areas at one time. Keep pushing the epoxy mix into the groove until it is just proud of the surrounding wood. Work it in so there are no voids from air bubbles. You can get creative by using removable temporary plugs in the circles you created so you can fill in intersecting lines. Then, after the lines inlay has cured, remove the temporary plug and do the circles in a different color.

Medallions on the inside bottoms of a big bowl can add additional drama. You can fill any cracks in the vessel to create dramatic effects. The sky is the limit to your creativity.

After the inlay has setup for at least 24-hours, clamp the work in the non-spinning lathe. You are setup for grinding. I have designed custom sanding disks to attach to my electric drill. Starting with 120 grit sandpaper on the sanding attachment slowly remove excess inlay material from the vessel. Do this with the lathe off, using a feathering motion slowly remove material until it is flush with the surrounding wood. Special care must be taken here to avoid gouging the surrounding wood. Once you have done this you can spin the piece and hand sand the inlay area with 220 thru 600-grit sandpaper. I find it is very helpful to vacuum the inlay clean to find any hidden voids. If necessary repair any voids with your original inlay mixture and sand flush. Prepare your piece for the final finish with a final sanding and do any painting with dyes at this time. Wait for your dyes to dry and sand any raised grain with 600-grit sandpaer. Vacuum all the excess dust and tack cloth the work. Always remember to wear safety glasses and dust mask while doing this work, safety is your job number one.

As a finish, I use a wipe-on food-safe salad bowl finish. It's wiped on and left to soak into the wood for several minutes, then lightly buffed to remove any excess. Let the finish harden for at least eight-hours. Repeat the process over several days to build up the varnish finish and buff using a sheepskin buffing wheel on your lathe until you reach the desired finish. Applying the finish is the most exciting part of the whole process; it is now that all your work pays off. As you apply your finish, the true beauty of the wood and your inlay work comes to life.

Do a good turn today and use inlays to reach a new level of creativity.

Author's Note: Bob shared the technique with us on how he uses temporary plugs of various sizes to create designs within the inlay. He uses dowels, plastic plugs, or any type of spacer, surrounds the edges in painter's tape and a little candle wax, then uses these devices to create negative areas within the wet inlay. Once the InLace has hardened, he uses a pair of pliers to remove the plug, and then fills in that space with another color inlay.

♥♥♥♥♥♥♥

Leah Reed: "InLaced Ostrich Egg"

Materials:

Ostrich egg (empty and as thick as possible), Simple napkin ring, InLace kit, InLace Thicken-it, InLace Buffing Compound, InLace Polishing Compound, hair spray, tracing paper, painter's tape, Masquenpen® or other resist, scroll saw pattern or drawing of own design, a large plastic coffee can or other container, bleach, and baking soda

Tools:

Red pen, Turbo carver or other high-speed carver, Orbital sander (such as Microlux® sander), Mini-carving burs, regular sandpaper (150/220/320 grit), wet-dry sandpaper (600/800/1500/2400/3200/4000/8000 and 12,000 grit), sandpaper cleaning stick

1. Place the Ostrich egg on the napkin ring and spray it with the hair spray. Apply three coats over the complete egg, letting it dry between coats. The hair spray stops any pencil or tracing paper markings from being absorbed into the eggshell. Eggs are very porous unlike a gourd.

A beautiful eagle design has been carved on this ostrich egg and then filled with black InLace. Leah has added interior lighting for a dramatic effect.

2. The eagle pattern was a copyright-free scroll pattern. If you are using a pattern, cut it out, leaving about a half-inch wide edge. Take the pattern and a piece of tracing paper and place it on the egg, using masking tape to secure it.

3. Trace the pattern on the egg with a red pen. The red helps so that you don't miss a section when tracing. Once completed, remove the pattern and tracing paper.

4. You are ready to begin carving. When carving, you want to be aware of the thickness of the egg. Ostrich eggs are about 3/32" thick. This gives you about 3/64" thickness for carving. If the pattern is a scroll pattern, reverse what the pattern says to carve, thus leaving the sections that a wood carver would normally carve out.

5. When you are done carving, take the egg and place it in the coffee container, with the hole facing up. Fill the container and the egg with bleach, leaving it for about 30 minutes. The purpose of this is to clean the inside, and outside, of the egg.

6. After the egg is bleached, remove the egg and empty the coffee container. Place the egg back into the container and fill it with water and about one-quarter of a cup of baking soda. Soak the egg for about 20 minutes. Remove the egg, rinse well and let dry.

7. Once the egg is dry, put Masquenpen on the eggshell that surrounds the carving. In the eagle design, it would be around the eye and feathers. Also apply about one-inch around the outer edge of the carved area. This helps guide you when sanding down the inlay.

8. It is ready to put the InLace into the carved section. Mix the InLace as directed (see the Mixing chapter in this book) and be sure to add some Thicken-it so that the resin will stay in the carving.

9. Once the InLace has cured, about 24-hours, begin sanding the design down with 150 grit sandpaper until you hit the Masquenpen resist. Continue sanding, with the Wet/Dry sandpaper, starting with 220 and going through 12,000. You can sand the complete egg if desired. Caution. When sanding the InLace with a rotary sander, the egg and sander will become very hot. If this happens, allow time for them to cool down or the InLace will become very gummy. To keep the sandpaper clean and to extend its use, use a sandpaper cleaning stick on a regular basis while sanding the egg and InLace.

10. Next, buff the InLace (and the whole egg, if you sanded it) with the InLace buffing compound.

11. Lastly, use the InLace polishing compound on the design (and entire egg, if sanded.)

Note: Visit Leah's web site, www.bluewhalearts.com, to see more of her egg and gourd art, for all the supplies required for this project, and for general gourd art supplies and equipment.

♥♥♥♥♥♥♥

Ronna Wuttke: "A Gourd with Character"

My first introduction to InLace was when my husband, David, handed me a can of resin and containers of dye, flakes, dust nuggets and granules, and some very sophisticated tools, pop sticks, and paper cups. He wanted me to make demos as he considered adding the product to our other art supplies at Turtle Feathers.

I wasn't sure what I was doing and part of my confusion was thinking that I needed to use all of the additives at the same time. I learned quickly that using too much can make a mixture overly thick and that used sparingly, the additives would enhance the InLace mixture.

Once I sorted out what to use and how much, I wanted to "test" the products out. I chose a gourd "basket" that cracked when it was cut, and after sewing it together, it looked very primitive. So I set out to make a simple and quick border as my first InLace project.

Using my Optima 2 carving unit, I carved the moat around the top of the gourd, making sure that my walls were straight and the carving had a little undercut to hold the inlay. I dug down fairly deep, but now I know that I really didn't need to dig to China, that a depth of one-eighth of an inch is sufficient.

Bonnie Gibson had posted some of her photos of the progression of the InLace process, and I was relieved to see that her pictures looked like my project…kind of messy. I had overfilled the inlay, in case of shrinking (now I know InLace doesn't shrink) and that some of the sticky mess I had made around the carving could be wiped off with fingernail polish remover.

Now I had to wait overnight for the inlay to harden. The next day, I wanted immediate satisfaction in reducing the inlay down to gourd skin level so I took out my big Makita® sander and let her rip. I had no great concerns for marring the gourd as my basket was already a piece with "character." I sanded quickly with medium grit sandpaper, creating a halo around the inlay. To help blend in the lines, I used Howard's Feed and Wax® to condition the gourd. (Now, several years later, the lines have blended and mellowed.)

So, with one piece under my belt, I was a pro, right? My next project was a turtle design on top of a wooden box. This time I didn't carve deep enough, so that when I sanded the inlay, the center of the turtle shell revealed the wood underneath the inlay. But sanding on wood alleviated the worry about removing the gourd skin. I traded one problem for another.

Now I was really ready! I chose a turtle design (again) and penciled it on a gourd. I carved and then used Terra InLace. I had also added small amounts of silver dust and teal nuggets to give the Terra a little more depth, but not enough to take away from the original color. Just before adding the hardener (I thought that I was being gypped because the bottle was only half-full, but there really is enough for the size can of InLace), I stirred the

mixture and found that I needed to add Thicken-it to make the mixture a little firmer. All the additives need to be incorporated into the mix before the hardener or activator is added. Finally, I carefully counted out the drops of hardener, filled in the carving, pushed and pulled the mix to break up any air bubbles, and then waited.

Once the inlay had hardened, I hand-sanded from coarse through very fine. The color of the inlay was very close to the gourd skin color, but I simply woodburned the areas around the resin **before** I used the buffing and polishing compounds. I wasn't sure what the effect might be in burning those products. And since I was woodburning, I didn't worry too much about removing some of the skin when sanding either. I then used both compounds on the inlay, hand-rubbing and also using a felt pad on the Optima at low speed. What a nice shine.

Another gourd artist, Randy Eckley, gave me some hints on preparing the carved area to accept InLace. He suggested woodburning along the walls of the inlay to "crisp" up the cut and to help angle the walls of the carving.

So through all my samples and mistakes, I learned what a great inlay material InLace can be, if used correctly. I liked most of my concoctions so I filed the mixtures in my "InLace Recipe Box" in case I wanted, or didn't want, to use the formula again.

Note: Be sure to find Ronna's Turtle in the photo Gallery, and visit Turtle Feathers' web site, www.turtlefeathers.net for more of Ronna's art, InLace products, and general gourd art supplies.

Ronna's gourd with "character" was saved from the scrap pile by a little creative stitching and a rim of InLace.

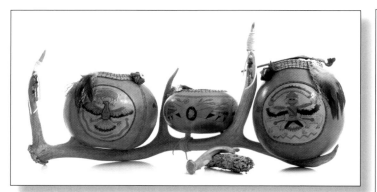

Priesthood of the Bow Zuni Ceremonial Bowls by Betsey Sloan.

Close up of the left hand on the bowl.

Close up of the right hand on the bowl.

Black necklace by Gloria Crane.

Turtle Bowl by Ronna Wuttke.

Oblong Lizard Clip by A. B. Amis.

Geisha by Betsey Sloan.

Carved Bowl by Gloria Crane.

Close-up of the detail on Crane's bowl.

Flowers on Black by Melinda Barrett.

49

Lighthouse on Ostrich Egg by Leah Reed.

Turtle and Bear Gourd Slices by A. B. Amis.

Buffalo, one of three designs, by Betsey Sloan.

Banded Bowl by Gloria Crane.

Cabochon by Jackie Jurecek.

InLaced Chief by Melinda Barrett.

Gourd Earrings by A. B. Amis.

Small Bowl by A. B. Amis.

Canteen with Dog Design by Leah Reed.

Broadbill Hummer by Bonnie Gibson.
Photography and copyright ® by Everett Gibson.

Warrior, Side 1, by Gary Devine

Warrior, Back Design.

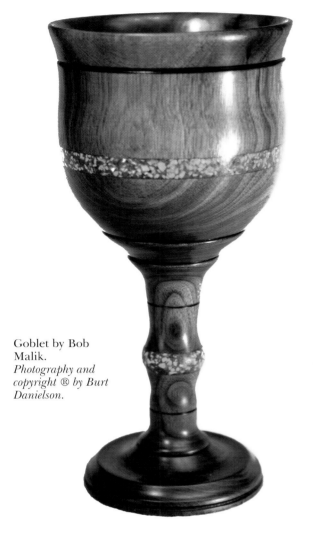

Goblet by Bob Malik.
Photography and copyright ® by Burt Danielson.

Five Suns Red by Randall Eckley.

Hopi Heaven & Earth by Randall Eckley.

Bottle Stoppers by Bob Malik.
Photography and copyright ® by Burt Danielson.

Geometric II by Randall Eckley.

Water and Wind by Bonnie Gibson.
Photography and copyright ® by Everett Gibson.

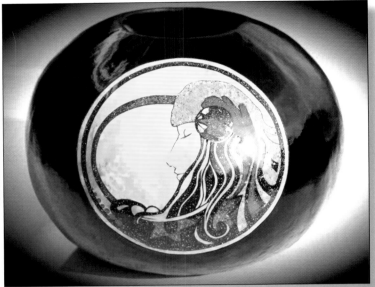

Moon Maiden II by Randall Eckley.

Wedding Gift by Randall Eckley.

Costa's Hummer by Bonnie Gibson.
Photography and copyright ® by Everett Gibson.

Vase, top detail.

Vase (close up of side) by Gary Devine.

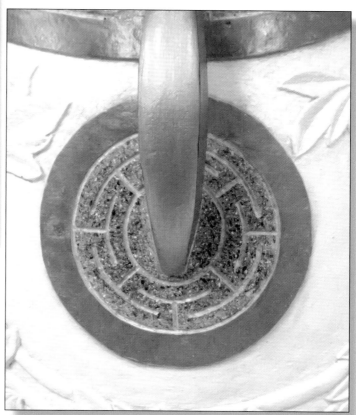

Vase, handle detail.

Bowl with Multiple Designs by Bob Malik.
Photography and copyright ® by Burt Danielson.

56

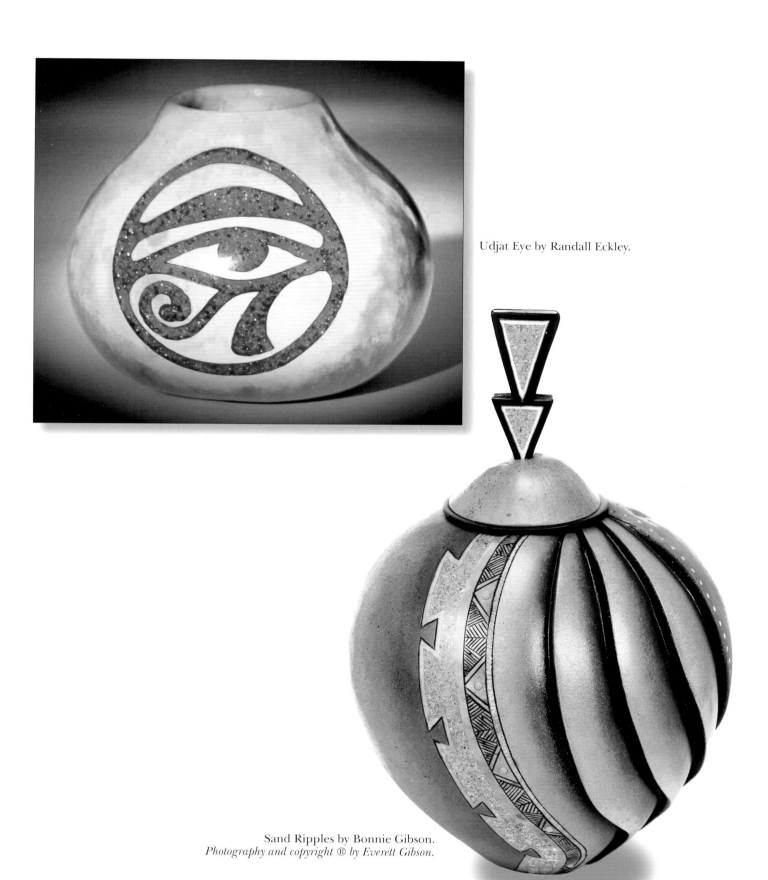

Udjat Eye by Randall Eckley.

Sand Ripples by Bonnie Gibson.
Photography and copyright ® by Everett Gibson.

ORIGINAL DESIGNS

Please feel free to use the following designs. The sunflower is an original design by Ronna Wuttke.
The InLace chief, dragonfly, Kokopelli, and dancing ladies are Betsey's original designs.

Sunflower

Kokopelli

Dragonfly

Dancing Ladies

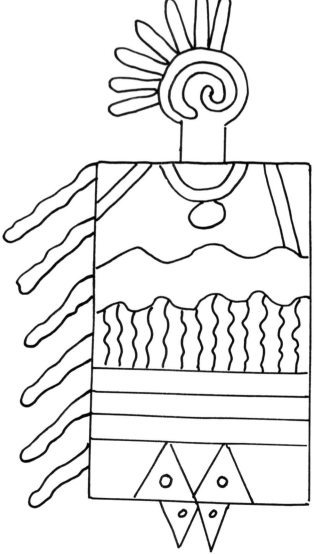

A. B. Amis
Email: AonlyBonly@msn.com

Although A. B. had dabbled a bit with sketching during a 35-year engineering career, it took retirement and gourds to get the right side of his brain really cranked up. Even now, an inclination toward orderliness and mathematical "correctness" is evident in his frequent use of repeating geometrical patterns in his carving. His introduction to chip carving was in a work-shop taught by Lyn Rohm at the Ohio gourd show in 1997, where he was strongly drawn to geometric carvings done by Lyn's father, Dr. Leslie Miller, an Ohio State math professor and gourd artist. (His work can be found in many private collections.). A. B. also enjoys challenging his new-found creativity by sculpting graceful pitchers and vessels from single gourds.

A charter member of the Florida Gourd Society, and "volunteered" by his wife, Frances, to be the Society's newsletter editor, A. B. also served terms as President and Show Chairman for a couple of years before turning the jobs over to others to allow him more time for indulging his own creativity, and for teaching others to carve and sculpt. He has taught workshops at gourd shows and festivals in Florida, Georgia, Alabama, Kentucky, Indiana, Missouri, North Carolina, and Mississippi, and has won numerous blue ribbons for his work at various shows.

A. B. and Frances live in a "Florida cracker" style home (tin roof, high ceilings, wide verandas) on five acres in the unincorporated fishing village of Grant, Florida, where they grow a few gourds and pass many pleasant hours crafting them on their spacious porches.

♥♥♥♥♥♥

Gloria Crane
Web Site: www.gloriousgourdcreations.com
Email: gloriousgourdcreations@verizon.net

Born in Los Angeles County in 1950, Gloria developed an enthusiasm for all sorts of art mediums at a very early age. As a child her favorite Christmas gifts were a brand new box of crayons, coloring books, and drawing paper.

Gloria has been married for thirty-eight years and has a son and daughter. She was able to take early retirement from the telecommunications field after twenty-six years of service. One morning, while watching a craft show on cable television, Gloria saw a gourd artist demonstrating her craft and knew immediately that she had to find out more about this natural and versatile canvas. That thirty-minute show led her to the Internet to research this new art form using gourds. Before she knew it, she was buying advance tickets to the CGS Gourd Festival at Welburn's Farm in Fallbrook, California. She took her first gourd lesson in February 2004 and was captivated.

Although accomplished as a self-taught artist in many mediums, Gloria has taken workshops from some of the finest and most sought after gourd artists available in California and Arizona, allowing her to bring a wealth of new techniques and skills to her already considerable artistic abilities.

Gourds offer Gloria the opportunity to carve, woodburn, weave, apply inlay as well as use paints, stains, and inks (often on the same piece) in the creation of her original and stunning gourd art. Her inspiration comes from her deep love of nature and animals, which is clearly evident in her work. She explains that she usually starts with an idea that has come during tranquil moments, but says she also keeps a pencil and sketchpad next to her bed for when she's awakened in the middle of the night with a design idea.

Always enthusiastic about sharing her passion and knowledge, Gloria is now teaching others in her home, at gourd festivals and at private venues.

♥♥♥♥♥♥

Gary Devine
Email: devine_c@hotmail.com

After finishing a degree in Science at the University of Western Ontario, Gary went to Hamilton Teachers' College where he discovered Art was his true interest and calling. As a result, he decided to continue on in the Fine Arts program at Western while teaching at the same time in the London, Ontario elementary school system. This led to achieving a major concentration in Fine Arts, and later, an Art Specialist Certificate. During 31 years of teaching to both children and adult groups, he has taught in full rotary situations, community and interest groups, and Ministry of Education courses.

Having worked with sculptural and flat-work pieces, Gary was intrigued by the possibilities with gourds. So, after retiring in 1999, he began experimenting. He has exhibited both in Canada and the United States, been included in books, and have won many awards including blue ribbons, Artistic Merit, President and Chairperson's Awards, and Best of Shows. His work primarily involves pyrography and/or carving, but he is always trying out 'new stuff.'

♥♥♥♥♥♥

Randall Eckley
Email: grahampaw@att.net

A self-taught gourd artist, Randy is a pharmacist by day. His artwork has garnered several awards and his inlay workshops draw artists from around the country.

His designs range from Art Deco, Architectural and Art Nouveau to Organic and Southwestern. Each piece is unique in style and design. Randy elevates the humble gourd to fine art, considering color, design, weight, interior treatments, and surface texture. All agree that the sense of touch is as important as the visual appeal of his pieces.

Randy, a.k.a. Gourdaholics's, most important contribution to the gourd art has been his use of epoxy resin inlay. The striking colors and mixtures transform the vessel into a focal point for the senses. His art pieces inspire a new appreciation for this truly atypical art form.

♥♥♥♥♥♥

Bonnie Gibson
Web Site: www.arizonagourds.com
Email: bonnie@arizonagourds.com

Bonnie Gibson is an accomplished artist in many forms of three-dimensional arts and fine crafts. Completely self-taught, she has gained recognition and awards for her work in gourds, wood carving, scrimshaw, and scale miniatures.

"I am a self taught artisan. I prefer this term over 'artist,' because to me it denotes a person who works with items that can be functional as well as aesthetically pleasing. Since I was a child, working with my hands and creating things captivated me. I took art classes in high school, but I always felt more comfortable with three-dimensional creations instead of traditional paintings and drawings."

"I discovered gourds quite by accident a few years ago, and immediately fell in love with them! Working with gourds allows me to utilize the technical skills that I've developed over the years working with

other media. I have lived in Arizona for almost thirty years, so interpreting some of the Native cultures and Southwestern designs is a favorite subject of mine."

Bonnie utilizes many tools and techniques to reach a finished design. Carving, pyrography, painting and inlays of stone make for striking accents to the overall design. Certain design elements such as carved sand ripples and basketry effects have become her signature patterns.

Bonnie's first gourd crafting book, *"Gourds: Southwest Gourd Techniques & Projects from Simple to Sophisticated,"* was published by Sterling Publishing in 2006. In addition to exploring a wide variety of tools, techniques, and gourd crafting information, the book includes over twenty projects with full color photographs and detailed step by step instructions. She has appeared in other gourd crafting books and has written numerous articles on gourd crafting.

Bonnie's work reflects the world that surrounds her; living in the southwest has provided her with an endless source of inspiration. One of Bonnie's primary goals is to help lift gourds out of the realm of "crafts" and into greater acceptance as fine art. To that end, she enjoys manipulating gourds in new ways, inviting the viewer to interpret them as something more while retaining their natural essence.

♥♥♥♥♥♥

Fonda Haddad
Email: Fonda-a-art@earthlink.net

Fonda Haddad is a professional fiber artist. She has a master's degree in Visual Arts Education and is a retired teacher who has taught kindergarten through college. Fonda had her own original clothing shop "The Fig Leaf," where she created and sold batik and silk painted clothing. Another thread that has run through her life is basketry, which she has created, taught, and sold for thirty years.

She is currently teaching at the John C. Campbell Folk School in North Carolina and Blue Ridge Mountain Arts Association in Georgia. She teaches at many gourd conferences including Florida, Georgia, North Carolina, Mississippi, Tennessee, and the Florida Tropical Weavers Guild State Conference. Her gourd work is for sale at the Frog and Dragon Art Gallery in Brasstown, North Carolina; her baskets may be found at the Georgia Mountain Fair with the Shooting Creek Basketry Guild or at Tapoka Lodge near Fontana Dam, and Sleepy Hollow Farm Store in Bryson City, North Carolina.

♥♥♥♥♥♥

Bob Malik
Email: bobmalik05@yahoo.com

Bob Malik of Witness Tree Products, Gettysburg, Pennsylvania, has been involved in the arts community all his life. Early in his career he studied fine arts and sculpture at the Brooklyn Museum. A native New Yorker, Bob was a commercial photographer for over 25 years. He has studied and worked at the New School University. A member of several associations, including the Northeastern Woodworkers Association and the Long Island Woodworkers Association, Bob has only been doing wood-turning since the early 1990s. He began turning after a seminar with master turner Ernie Conover.

The turned bowls, goblets, and other pieces Malik handcrafts all come from old growth trees from historic sites in and around Gettysburg. Malik believes trees bear witness to so many magnificent events in our lives, hence the name Witness Tree. "I like to think that in some little way I'm preserving our heritage one tree at a time." Each piece of wood has some characteristic that makes it interesting and unique. Celebrating the contributions the wood has to offer, Malik works the wood's imperfections into the piece he's making. If there are cracks, he might choose to make them slightly bigger and use a decorative inlay to strengthen the area.

Much of Malik's work is influenced by the Southwest. The "Southwest Collection" includes the brilliant hues of turquoise and bright reds painted with aniline dyes. The rustic work of well-known furniture maker Thomas Molesworth inspired his "Cowboy Art Series."

In addition to the blue-green turquoise of his Southwest line, Malik uses other colors and textures, often including a metallic material, such as brass filings to add sparkle. Each piece he creates allows him to experiment with more options. The "Naturals Series" includes the actual bark, inclusions, and holes from the tree. The "Civil War Collection" incorporates the uniform buttons of the Civil War era. The "Renaissance Collection" was inspired by medieval pewter and pottery. Painting with aniline dyes using cloisonné techniques has added a burst of color to the work; inlays with stone blends, metals, and turquoise beads all enhance the natural beauty of the wood.

Recovering from the post-traumatic effects of 9/11 in New York City, Bob embraced his art's therapy to create a future. In February 2006, he made his way to Gettysburg and the unique entertainment venue known as Patriot Point Village, a community of several distinct venues including Witness Tree, Regimental Quartermaster, The Jeweler's Daughter, Battlefield Guides Association.

♥♥♥♥♥♥♥

Leah Reed
Web Site: www.bluewhalearts.com
Email: leah@bluewhalearts.com

Leah has been working with gourds and eggs since 2000. She is a national award-winning gourd and egg artist. Although initially self-taught, she has studied with nationally renowned artists. Her techniques include carving, dyes, inks, woodburning, oil pencils, coiling, and rim ornamentation.

She started Blue Whale Arts, LLC in 2004 selling her fine art at local shows, galleries, and through her website, www.bluewhalearts.com. Because she found it very frustrating that the supplies needed for working with these mediums were not easily found locally, she expanded the business to include selling those tools. She also teaches gourd classes in her home, at gourd festivals, and private venues.

She is passionate about bringing awareness to gourd and egg art in the New England area and has organized the last two New England Gourdvine gatherings and is the moderator of the NEGourdvine Yahoo Group.

Born and raised in Salem, New Hampshire, Leah attributes her passion for the arts to her mother who always had an art project she was creating on the kitchen table. Leah lives New Hampshire with her husband of twenty-three years. They have raised three children and have eight grandchildren. They travel with their three Mini Dachshunds to the different gourd shows.

At their homestead in Epping, New Hampshire, they raise peacocks, geese, doves, American Fantail Pigeons, and Golden Red Pheasants, collecting, washing, and hand-dying the feathers that are then offered for sale. They gather many of the natural materials they sell from their yard, or collect them throughout their travels, baking them to ensure that they are pest free. They grow a variety of gourds on a small scale to have available to students.

Leah is known by her family and friends as the "Egg lady out of her gourd, who has gone to the birds."

♥♥♥♥♥♥♥

Ronna Wuttke
www.turtlefeathers.net
Email: david@turtlefeathers.net

Ronna Wuttke is a self-taught artist who enjoys working with multi-mediums, especially those that interact well with nature.

Formally a pre-school special needs teacher for twenty years, she now spends most of her time with her husband, David, as proprietors of their business, Turtle Feathers, based in North Carolina.

She recently established a gourd museum with over six hundred pieces of gourd art. Ronna is an international award winner and has been teaching gourd art classes for about ten years.

Most of her work reflects her love for nature and her passion for the Native American people. Each gourd is a piece of history, reflecting the life of our ancient ancestors that she wants to keep alive.

While this is not a complete list of gourd art suppliers, it is a list of those I use most often and that carry the products, tools, and equipment found throughout this book. The photographer for most of the images in this book is also listed.

Turtle Feathers

David and Ronna Wuttke, www.turtlefeathers.net

InLace family of products; Proxxon, Microlux, and Optima tools, bits, rotary sander, and sanding discs; fade resistant leather dyes, QuikWood, graphite paper, Angelus acrylic leather paint, and many more art supplies for the gourd artist.

Blue Whale Arts

Leah Reed, www.bluewhalearts.com

General gourd art supplies and tools including dust collectors, burs, smaller-sized respirators, sanding sticks, Micro-mesh 3" sanding disc kits (600-12000 grit), Ostrich eggs and all the supplies required to work with them, embellishments, and inlays from around the world plus hand-dyed feathers and pine needles.

Bonnie Gibson

www.arizonagourds.com

Foredom carvers, numerous bits, woodcarving and woodburning tools, embellishments, beads, drum and musical supplies, gourd books, tutorials, monthly newsletter, and much more.

Mardi Gourds

Mary and Dick Segreto, www.mardigourds.com

General gourd art tools, supplies and equipment, a complete line of environmentally friendly dyes, paints, gels and finishes, books, tutorials, and stamping and scrapbooking supplies.

Primitive Originals

Kathy and Bob James, www.primitiveoriginals.com

Extensive line of gourd craft supplies, tools and equipment, including hand-held KumiHimo KumiLoom, books, Washi paper, beads and bones, books, and more.

The Caning Shop

Jim Widess, www.thecaningshop.com

Your source for supplies, tools, and books for gourd crafters, basket makers, and chair caning.

Betsey Sloan

www.thepodlady.com

Pods and dried botanicals from around the world, deer antlers, dried sea urchins and starfish, coiled cane, and more, for use as gourd rim embellishments or for general arts and crafting.

Timeless Memories

Jennifer Van Allen

Email: timeless@ftc-i.net

Photography, business cards, posters, custom cards, and bookmarks.